# A SPY AT HAMPTON COURT

*Kit Scarlett Mysteries
Book Three*

Adele Jordan

*Also in the Kit Scarlett Series*
The Gentlewoman Spy
The Royal Assassin
The Lost Highlander
The Traitor Queen

# A SPY AT HAMPTON COURT

Published by Sapere Books.

24 Trafalgar Road, Ilkley, LS29 8HH

saperebooks.com

Copyright © Adele Jordan, 2022

Adele Jordan has asserted her right to be identified as the author of this work.
All rights reserved.

No part of this publication may be reproduced, stored in any retrieval system, or transmitted, in any form, or by any means, electronic, mechanical, photocopying, recording, or otherwise, without the prior written permission of the publishers.
This book is a work of fiction. Names, characters, businesses, organisations, places and events, other than those clearly in the public domain, are either the product of the author's imagination, or are used fictitiously.
Any resemblances to actual persons, living or dead, events or locales are purely coincidental.

ISBN: 978-1-80055-891-5

# CHAPTER 1

*Nottingham Castle, 1585*

"Not enough like a man, eh?" Kit Scarlett muttered, repeating the words that had been whispered to her minutes before. She looked around, half expecting the man who had said them to reappear, but he was gone, safely hidden, now that she was so close to the castle.

Kit hesitated as she lifted her eyes to the castle gatehouse. Vast, with two great towers either side of the gate, she rather thought it a castle built for a giant, with a door so tall there would have to be five of her standing on each other's shoulders to reach the top. The turrets stretched so wide and round that she couldn't even see their edges, just the gleaming, almost white stone turning slowly orange in the setting sun.

Kit and her Scottish espionage partner, Iomhar, had been sent on another mission by Queen Elizabeth's spymaster, Sir Francis Walsingham. The mission was to speak to one of the prisoners, a woman who had a message for Walsingham. A message she said pertained to the safety of England's throne.

"Not enough…" Kit murmured again, pulling her hat lower. The woollen cap bore a jackdaw's feather today, plain and black, befitting the low status she was trying to adopt. As she turned up the collar around her neck against the evening chill, the white linen chafed against her neck and chin. "Then I will do something about it."

She turned away from the gatehouse, knowing she would be irritating her partner, who was awaiting her somewhere nearby, no doubt peering between the groups of men that hovered by the alehouse across the path, each one drunkenly leaning against the other. Kit turned her focus to the carts being unloaded in front of the gatehouse, which bore all kinds of dead birds ready for feasting.

"A lot of food for a prison," Kit said to herself as she moved to the edge of a cart. In the road, the wheels had scored marks into the dirt, thick and ridge-like, kicking up speckles on the cobbles nearby. Checking over her shoulder to ensure no one was watching her, Kit bent down and took a handful of earth, then straightened up and dabbed it along her chin.

All she needed was a thin covering, enough to make her appear as some filthy worker, so that no guard would wish to look at her for too long. With the dirt aptly applied, she turned toward the gatehouse as one of the horses attached to the cart began to whinny. Kit stepped to the side as the horse evacuated its bowels on the cobbles beside her boots. Her nose wrinkled in distaste before she alighted on an idea. No one would look too closely at her if they were trying to avoid her.

Delving a hand into the pocket of her grey woollen trousers, she pulled out a white cloth. She shook it loose as she checked everyone close to her was busy. They were all focused on carrying the delivered food into the castle; not one glanced her way.

Bending down to the manure, she used the cloth to take a handful of the stinking mass and tied it up, before pocketing it. Her eyes stung against the stench, but it clearly did its job for as she moved toward the back of the cart, the driver passed by her quickly, grumbling under his breath.

"Stinking lads, don't know how to wash themselves."

Kit smiled and moved to the cart beside her. There were two barrels on the back, small enough to be carried. She lifted one onto her shoulder, using it to hide her face on one side, and followed the other numerous delivery lads towards the gatehouse.

The cobbles began to slant up toward the turrets, where a tall portcullis had been raised within the body of the building. Only its lethal points were visible, hanging down from the top of the gateway. Beneath these points there were three guards, each one instructing the delivery boys in harsh tones where to place the food.

"Birds in kitchens," the first guard said with a strong Nottinghamshire accent, gesturing over his head. "You there, the one with the barrel."

"Me?" Kit asked, jerking her head up as she reached his side.

"We don't need beer. We have our malthouse for that." He shook his head, his grey eyes thinning to slits with suspicion.

"It's mead, sir, not beer." Kit avoided his gaze, barely peering beneath the lip of her cap.

"Ergh, you stink." The guard reeled backwards, wafting a hand in front of his face.

Kit bit her lip, trying hard to stop the smile. "I'll be quick, sir. In and out before you know it." She walked straight past him, following the other young lads who were already carrying in the dead birds.

"Kitchens! With the others."

"Yes, sir," Kit called back, though she didn't look around. She kept the barrel chiefly over her face on one side, using it as a shield as she followed the others across the inner courtyard. They moved like a trail of ants, each one following the other in the dying evening light, toward a door set in a thick curtain wall. When two more guards walked past Kit, she moved the barrel to her other shoulder, keeping her face hidden.

"Time to act," she whispered to herself as they moved closer to the kitchens.

Far ahead, she could see the main keep of the castle, where around the back more guards were gathered together, suggesting they had something to watch over. It had to be the dungeons. She lowered the barrel from her shoulder as she followed the other lads into the kitchens. The place was a raucous affair with many cooks working in a small space, and lots of birds placed over the fire on a spit. One of the cooks bemoaned the delivery, wondering how he was supposed to serve up so much food in one feast for the sheriff and his men in such a short amount of time.

"You, put the barrel there." One of the cooks gestured at Kit, pointing down beside the fireplace. Kit did as she was asked and turned back round, only to find the cook now shooing her away. "Off with you."

Kit scuttled to the door, though she couldn't leave yet. Seeing some of the delivery boys had gone, and others were still piling up the birds on a table opposite the fire, she took her chance. She needed a distraction.

Inching towards the fireplace, she waited for the boy turning the spit to look away, quenching his thirst with a tankard that had been placed beside him. She then knocked the spit with her elbow and hastened away. The spit fell into the fire, casting with it the cooking birds, which instantly set alight.

"Ho! What happened here?" a voice cried out.

"Boy! You been shirking your duty."

A mad scramble was made for the spit, and there was an attempt to recover the birds, with everyone turning their backs on the doors that led out of the kitchen. Kit took her opportunity and instead of taking the door through which she had come in, she took the other. She found herself in a narrow corridor, so tight that she thought it must have been hard for the portly cook to walk through such a space.

Heading along the passage, Kit never slowed her pace, not until she reached a door that bore a small opening within the wooden slats. It allowed her to peer out to another courtyard. This cobbled square was placed against the curtain wall that overlooked the fortifications on one side. Guards still paced back and forth, all there to watch the two small doors that marked the entrance to the dungeons. The doors were a clear indication of the prisoners beyond, for they were heavily barred and the guards leaned purposefully against them.

It didn't take long for the cries of the trouble in the kitchens to reach the courtyard. One guard came hurrying around the building and across a path to join the others, gesturing over his shoulder.

"One of the delivery lads has dropped our food in the fire."

"That's our feast gone, then," another sighed, turning his focus back to the door.

"Shirking your duty again, Myers? We're ordered to find him for a beating." The first grabbed the second's shoulder, pushing him forward, urging the others to follow. One or two guards hung back, looking rather reluctant to abandon their posts, but hearing it had been ordered by a captain, they soon hurried on, leaving the courtyard empty.

Kit pushed open the door behind which she had been hiding, peering around the edge to check if there was anyone still in the courtyard. It was empty, with nothing but jackdaws cawing above her on the ramparts, as if trying to alert their masters to her presence. Kit shot them one resentful glance before she took off across the courtyard, heading straight for the dungeon doors.

She hovered between them for a second, uncertain which door to take. Then she heard shouts coming from within.

Beyond the door on her left, a woman cried, "Get off me, Sampson!"

A loud slap followed the words, skin hitting skin, then a wail of pain.

Kit took her chances and reached for the door to this dungeon. The iron handle twisted uncomfortably in her grasp, suggesting it was aged and slowly breaking. Bending down to get through the short doorway, Kit found she was not within the curtain wall at all. The dungeon was carved into the rock beneath her, with stairs dropping away at such a steep angle that she nearly tripped.

Hearing the argument was still taking place somewhere further away in the dungeon, Kit closed the door behind her and crept down the stone steps, moving on the toes of her boots. The further she moved down the stairwell, the darker it became. What little light had been filtering through the gaps around the door faded completely, until she had to feel her way down the last few steps, placing her hands against the walls on either side of her.

When she reached the bottom of the staircase, her body jolted with surprise before her hand found another door. This one was set flush into the wall, and only a dim orange glow seeped through the slits between the door and its frame. In the dark, she felt for a handle, scrambling for a minute before the door eventually opened.

On the other side the dungeon was revealed to be little more than a carved-out cave — a rounded alcove with pillars in the middle where the stone had been chipped away. In front of a single dungeon space there was a grate with thick iron slats that reached from floor to ceiling, and a small, padlocked door, barely discernible from the bars.

"They're back," one of the voices from the dungeon grumbled as Kit stepped forward, her eyes restlessly searching the space.

On Kit's side of the iron grate, there were three candles, their small flames offering little light so far beneath ground. On the other side, the dungeon was filthy and stank almost as much as she did. The carved walls were half hidden by a handful of people, each one fighting for their own space. The faces were all turned toward her, as if waiting to see what she would do. She tried not to wrinkle her nose as she looked between them, noticing the way some of the men scratched at their hair and clothes, bothered by lice. Another man stood from where he had been using the privy — a hole in the stone.

"Who you think 'e 'as come for?" one of the figures asked, elbowing another beside them.

"Sampson, do not touch me again." The woman's voice rang out, making Kit snap her gaze in her direction.

She stood out as not belonging. Dressed in as poor clothes as those around her, she was the only woman, standing as close to the iron grating as she possibly could, with her fingers latched around the bars and her temple resting against them. The dark brown hair that must have once been rather fine and well-kept was straggly with sweat and dirt. Her cheeks were speckled with something so dark brown in colour that Kit felt herself gag.

When the prisoner behind the woman reached out for her arm another time, she elbowed him sharply in the gut. He backed away, much to the amusement of the other prisoners, clearly not intending to defy her another time.

Kit moved to stand next to the woman, staring at her face and waiting for her to respond. It took a minute for the woman to realise just where Kit was standing, for she was so lost in thought, murmuring under her breath and gripping the bars until her knuckles turned white. Eventually, her blue eyes flicked up to Kit, widening at her coming so close.

"Praying?" Kit asked, never moving as she spoke. "I do not suppose it has done you much good so far."

The woman frowned a little more. "You are a…"

"I know," Kit said, nodding. She hadn't deepened her voice; it would be plain enough for this stranger to see that Kit was a woman. "Maybe instead of talking to the divine, you should ask someone living for help." Kit gestured at her own body, making the woman tilt her head.

"Who are you?"

"I cannot answer that now," Kit murmured, looking toward the other prisoners that were watching her closely. "Miss Georgiana Meadows?"

"Yes," the woman said quietly, her lips barely moving.

"You wished to deliver a message. To a certain person." Kit offered a smile, knowing she couldn't say more.

"He received my letter?" Miss Meadows asked, her eyebrows raised.

"He did." Kit shifted her boots on the cobbles, looking back at the door through which she had come. She knew her distraction would not have worked for long. She only had a short time to speak to Miss Meadows before she would have to make her escape, probably by a different route to how she had entered. "What is your message for him?"

"You expect me to utter it here?" Miss Meadows laughed. It was a rather sickly laugh that did not befit her, as if she was lacking the strength that she was accustomed to.

"I am here at your request. Not my own." Kit spoke slowly. She had come because Walsingham had needed her to.

Nothing more. "Why would you send for us if you did not want to share your message?"

"You do not understand. What I have to tell you depends on a deal."

"A deal? What kind of deal?" Kit asked.

As Miss Meadows opened her mouth to speak again, Sampson the prisoner stretched toward her. She turned round and stamped hard on his foot, making him cry out in pain.

"Shh!" Kit warned, looking back at the door. She feared it would open and that a guard would come running.

"They will not come. They never come. Even if we scream that someone is dying of starvation."

Kit winced at Miss Meadows' words and turned back to her. "What deal did you want?"

"You want what I have to tell you? Then you must do something for me first."

"Why would I do that?" Kit asked with a shrug. "How do I know that what you have to tell us is even worth something?"

"It is!"

"I can hardly take your word as a guarantee of that, can I?" Kit said, holding the woman's gaze. Miss Meadows clearly faltered, her lips parting wordlessly. The candles in the room basked her pale face in an orange glow, highlighting the gauntness of it. "If you have nothing to tell me, then I will take my leave."

Kit turned and headed to the door with speed. She had her fingers on the iron handle when Miss Meadows spoke again, her voice rushed and high pitched.

"It pertains to the queen." Her words made the prisoners behind her whisper, as if they were tittering at some ditty being performed by travelling players in the town square.

"I do not think your new friends believe you," Kit pointed out as she turned, hooking her thumbs into the pockets of her buckskin trousers.

"They are no friends of mine," Miss Meadows said, jerking her head at the other prisoners and offering Sampson one more warning look. "She is ill, is she not?"

Kit lurched forward, moving so quickly that she nearly tripped on the ridges in the carved stone. "How do you know that?" she asked in a whisper. Walsingham and the privy council had worked hard to keep it a secret. No one else knew; they viewed it as their way of keeping the country at peace. After all, how would the people react when they found out their queen was sick, and she had no heir to take her place?

Miss Meadows smiled for the first time, as if she sensed her victory. "You want to know what I have to tell you, then here is our deal." She glanced at the prisoners, turning up her nose at the state of them before she faced Kit, pressing so close against the bars that she made red ridges in her cheeks. "Help me to escape this place, and I will tell you what I know."

# CHAPTER 2

Kit knew she didn't have long to think. She glanced at the door, aware that she had minutes until they were discovered.

"Well?" Miss Meadows demanded.

"You keep to this deal," Kit warned as she delved a hand inside her doublet, tearing open one of the laces to reach a secretly sewn pocket, "or I will bring you back here."

Miss Meadows nodded without blinking, clearly taking Kit's warning seriously.

Kit took a small compass out of her pocket and lifted the brass lid. It was so dark in that dungeon that it was impossible to see where the needle was pointing on the ivory dial, but that wasn't why she needed the device. Taking hold of the spindle, she lifted the compass face clean out of the case, aware that Miss Meadows and the other inmates were eying her closely. Turning her back on them, she retrieved the small vial she needed and held it up to the candlelight, twisting it and watching as the black powder slid up and down.

"I pray this works," she muttered to herself, closing the compass back up and hiding it in her pocket once more. Hastening to the lock in the bars of the cell, she pulled out the small cork in the vial and tipped the powder into the lock opening.

"What are you doing?" Miss Meadows asked, moving to stand behind the barred door.

"You wish to be free, Miss Meadows? Then step back from this door. As far as you can."

Miss Meadows heeded her words, scurrying so far into the corner that the other inmates scuffled that way too, their eyebrows raising and their lips muttering. Kit moved towards the candles. Beside them were spent parchments, each one with an untidy scrawl across the top, detailing the inmates' names. She found the sheet bearing Miss Meadows' name and rolled it up, making a long, thin spill. Using one of the candles, she then lit the end, watching as the yellow flame took hold, tall and willowy, as if it were a dancing figure.

"Cover your ears," Kit whispered as she moved toward the bars.

"What are you doing?" one of the inmates asked, inching toward the gate.

"Step away if you hope to keep your eyebrows." Kit gave no other warning. She stuffed the lit paper in the lock and jumped away, turning her back.

It took only a second for the gunpowder to be lit and take effect — a bang ricocheted through the dungeon, shaking the bars as the lock cracked open, with sparks shooting out of it. The candles behind them shuddered in the aftermath.

"What was that?"

"Gunpowder."

The inmates talked amongst themselves as they slowly unfurled their arms and uncovered their faces.

"Did it work?" Miss Meadows cried, not moving from where she cowered on the other side of the cell.

Kit stepped forward and kicked hard at the door, aiming the heel of her boot an inch below the lock. It swung open, with what remained of the lock clattering and echoing around them.

"It looks like you are all free. For now." Kit beckoned Miss Meadows forward.

"That was not what I asked." Miss Meadows seemed unnerved, glancing over her shoulder at the other inmates who were hurrying after her, each one pulling their rags tighter around their bodies.

"Pandemonium, Miss Meadows. It is the easiest way to cover an escape." Kit shrugged, as if the answer were an obvious one. When Miss Meadows stepped out of the cell, Kit reached for her wrist, pulling her forward.

"Ow!"

"Listen attentively. If we are to escape from here without being caught, then you are my shadow. Where I go, you must follow, yes?"

"Yes." Miss Meadows' brow was furrowed as Kit led her toward the door, with the other inmates following. "If you work for *him*, why could you not just ask them to release me?"

"You think that would work?" Kit scoffed as she swung open the door, leading the way back to the steps as she dragged Miss Meadows behind her. "Enough talk. We must be silent."

She wasn't going to explain to Miss Meadows that she did not have the authority to take her out of that dungeon. Even if Walsingham had given permission, she knew well enough that the sheriff of the castle would have issues with the idea of releasing one of their own when requested.

"This place plays by its own rules," Kit murmured as she took the steps back up through the carved rock toward the dungeon door, with Miss Meadows' feet slipping on the steps behind her. When she reached the top, the inmates were impatient to leave, each one gnashing their teeth like animals prepared to kill. Kit opened the door an inch, peering out through the gap and into the streak of light to see that the guards were back in their place, standing perfectly still in the middle of the corridor. Each one was twisting their neck around, questioning what had been the source of that loud bang.

"This is an escape?" Miss Meadows said impatiently. Kit waved a hand sharply in her direction, again calling for silence. A second later, her lip curled as an idea formed.

"You desire your freedom?" Kit whispered to the inmates. "Take it." With one hand on Miss Meadows, she dragged her back into the shadows behind the door, and with the other, she thrust it open, giving the inmates their chance.

As one, they ran forward, blinking in the light, until some skidded to a halt on the cobbles, seeing the guards that were awaiting them. Kit kept the door ajar as she watched through the gap created by the hinges.

"They're out!" one of the guards cried, pointing round with a pike.

The other guards did not need telling twice. They ran toward their prisoners, who promptly took off in all directions, each one trying to make their escape from the castle.

"Stop! Grab them before they reach the gate." Shouts and bellows went up from around the castle as the courtyard quickly emptied. Each guard took a prisoner and pursued him as he ran around the compound.

"Now," Kit murmured to Miss Meadows, pulling her into a now empty courtyard. Her eyes darting to the battlements on the walls, Kit could see they had quickly emptied too, with each guard running toward the portcullis. Miss Meadows strained to break free of Kit's grasp as she attempted to follow the guards. "Where are you going?" Kit asked, tightening her hold.

"To the gate! Where do you think?"

"You think you can escape that way?" Kit shook her head, tugging on Miss Meadows' wrist so strongly that she pulled her back in the opposite direction. "I heard you were cleverer than that." Miss Meadows huffed in response, still struggling in her effort to be free. "Are you not the woman who has been sending coded messages to France? Asking for an army to arrive?"

"Your tone suggests I was in the wrong, but yes."

Kit cursed as she towed Miss Meadows toward the curtain wall. At the side of the courtyard there were barrels pushed together, waiting to be opened for the feast later that day. Kit bent toward them, smelling the ale through the wood, before she reached for the rope that bound the barrels together.

"If you want your freedom, do not run now." Kit's words were enough to keep Miss Meadows in place as she released her wrist, using both hands to unwind the rope from the barrels.

"What are you doing?"

"Finding another way out that does not use the main gate." Kit wrapped the rope over her shoulder before taking Miss Meadows' wrist again, urging her toward a set of stone steps that led up the wall onto the battlements. Miss Meadows slipped more than once, nearly falling onto her knees. "Watch where you are putting your feet." Kit reached back, hurrying her up the steps on her toes.

"I am watching for the guards!" Miss Meadows replied in a panicked whisper.

"Then be faster with your feet, so they cannot catch you."

Reaching the battlements, Kit pushed Miss Meadows to the very edge of the wall and leaned over the staggered crenelations. Peering down, Kit could make out a steep drop where the ground gave way to a short stack of caves, a malthouse and a path. It was not particularly high, but high enough to make Miss Meadows' nails crunch against the top of the wall.

"This will do," Kit said hurriedly as she unfastened the rope from her shoulder and wrapped it tightly around one of the crenelations, knotting it so harshly that the rope strained against the stone.

"What will do?" Miss Meadows asked, backing up from the wall.

"That is the wrong way," Kit said with a small smile, pointing behind Miss Meadows. In the distance, shadows were beginning to move against the wall, suggesting the guards were returning to their posts.

"What do you expect us to do? Climb down?" Miss Meadows whispered frantically, waving her arms as she moved back toward Kit.

"Which would you rather face?" Kit asked, gesturing to the shadows. She didn't waste any more time arguing and climbed up onto the wall, wrapping the rope around her waist.

"Damn your blood," Mis Meadows muttered, climbing onto the wall on her knees and scraping her skirt across the stone.

"Yours too." Kit instructed Miss Meadows to turn round and take hold of the rope. "I will go first; follow closely."

"Have you done this before?" Miss Meadows asked, not moving as Kit began to climb down.

"Oh yes," Kit said with a smile. "From much higher, too." The memory of when she had climbed down from Edinburgh Castle's walls was stark in her mind. "Now." She used her feet to hop down the wall, aided by the tension of the rope. Miss Meadows followed, but at a distance, struggling not to let out small squeals. "Shh!" Kit ordered, to little effect.

By the time Kit reached the ground and unwound the rope from her waist, Miss Meadows had barely reached halfway.

Kit's arrival made one old man jump. He was sitting not far from where she landed, with his hat in front of him, evidently spending his days begging. A letter had been burned into his temple: 'v' for vagrant.

"Good morning," Kit said, affecting nonchalance as she tipped her cap to him. He smiled a little, seemingly intrigued until his face fell and he pointed upwards. Kit followed his gesture to see Miss Meadows was slipping off the rope. "God's wounds!" She slipped completely, tumbling to the ground in such a kerfuffle that Kit had to reach out and grab her, barely catching her under the arms before her head could hit the ground.

"Ow — my feet!" Miss Meadows complained as she tore herself from Kit's grasp, curling into a bundle on the floor. Her feet had hit the ground with a heavy thud. "I do not remember asking for near death as we escaped."

"You should have been more particular in your request, then." Kit reached down, grabbing Miss Meadows' arm and hauling her to her feet. "We do not have time for conversation." Looking back up to the battlements, she could see a guard had found their rope and was peering at it, clearly suspicious. It was becoming obvious that someone had escaped.

Kit crossed to where the begging man was sitting in his rags, before she delved into her pocket and flipped him a coin. He caught it with a mad reach of his hands, snatching it from the air.

"May I…?" she asked, lifting one of his rags from the earth. It was a cloak of some kind, torn and tatty. The man nodded and kissed the coin in thanks.

"Put this on." Kit wrapped the cloak around Miss Meadows' shoulders and steered her away, urging her to skirt round the castle and climb the hill, back toward the gate.

"Where are we going?" Miss Meadows demanded, driving her heels into the soil. "You are taking me back."

"No, but there is someone we must meet."

Kit stopped a short distance from the gate, her eyes flicking between the market and the guards that were on the other side of the lowered portcullis. They had hold of the inmates that had attempted their escape, dragging them back toward their dungeons. Kit smiled a little — her plan had worked, and the convicts had not escaped. Bar one.

Between the market-goers, she couldn't see who she was looking for. She turned back to Miss Meadows, flicking the collar of the cloak up to hide her face. Kit then whistled into the air. It was a short ditty, 'Leave Lightie Love', a tune she and her partner had heard on their return from Northumberland in the streets of York. It hadn't left their minds since. Buoyant and high, it was easy to recognise. She whistled the main chorus once and then fell silent, with Miss Meadows looking up at her with narrowed eyes.

"What are you doing?"

"Would you believe me if I said I was struck by a mood to make merry and sing?" Kit asked.

"Aye, that's a wee voice. Next time, whistle louder, Kit," a voice replied, as familiar to Kit as her own. "I couldn't hear ye above the bellowing of the guards. Does that have something to do with ye?"

Kit turned her head to see Iomhar at her side, hardly recognisable in the poor man's weaves he was wearing — a tunic and a pair of long trousers, with a bag slung over his shoulder. He looked as any other stall holder might, aside from the belt at his waist and the pistol handle that was just about visible.

"Perhaps," Kit said, pulling Miss Meadows forward for Iomhar to see. At once, his expression darkened, his green eyes narrowing.

"Ye helped her escape? That was not the order."

"Since when do you care about what *he* orders us to do?" Kit asked.

Iomhar shrugged. "Aye, ye'd be right."

"She will not tell us her message unless we get her out of here."

"Then ye best make her climb on that cart." Iomhar moved forward and gestured to an empty cart at the edge of the road. "We'll take her beyond the city walls."

Miss Meadows went eagerly this time, no longer needing to be dragged around by Kit. She struggled to clamber up, though, prompting Kit and Iomhar to share an exasperated look. Kit quickly took hold of her, levering her onto the back, where she fell amongst bundles of hay.

"Puh!" Miss Meadows spat out strands of straw as Kit climbed up beside her. "This is not the way a lady travels."

"You lost the right to travel finely when you sent those letters to the King of France. Consider yourself lucky *he* did not ask for you to be brought to the Tower." Kit's words made Miss Meadows scramble further back in the cart with fear. They all knew who she was talking of, without Kit having to utter his name. The spymaster was known so well these days that not even a code was needed to refer to him.

The cart jolted forward as Iomhar clambered into the driver's seat and flicked the reins of the one pony that was leading them. They moved slowly through the streets, past the market-goers and between timbered houses, mottled with white. When they passed through the city gates, Iomhar nodded easily at the guard, who didn't even attempt to stop them. He merely waved them on their way, leaving Miss Meadows to look about, her head twisting back and forth.

"Do not look too amazed," Kit said in a low voice. "You will draw attention to us."

Miss Meadows did her best to sit perfectly still as Iomhar drove down a smaller road away from the city, pebbled at the edges and with deep trenches left in the earth by carts that had passed through. He pulled to a stop beside a dip in the road, hidden from the city gates by a bank of trees.

"Well?" Kit sat forward off one of the hay bales, piercing Miss Meadows with a glare as the trees behind them shivered in the wind.

"I am free?" Miss Meadows asked in disbelief.

"For now," Iomhar said carefully as he turned in the cart seat to look at their charge. "What is your message? Or we take ye back again."

"Tell us how you also know the queen is sick," Kit ordered, her voice harsh. She could feel Iomhar's sudden look; he was equally startled that this prisoner knew.

"I heard men talking," Miss Meadows murmured as she climbed down, eager to escape for good.

"Where?" Iomhar asked.

"In York. I was delivering one of my letters to a messenger in a tavern when I heard them. They said she was sick, but that it was not enough."

"What was not enough?" Iomhar asked, leaping down from the cart and landing in the road with muddy splatters around his boots. Miss Meadows scrambled back, nearly colliding with him before she peered over the edge of the cart, looking at Kit.

"Not enough for her death. They were discussing a plot to see her dead."

"What plot?" Kit asked fiercely, growing impatient.

"Gunpowder." Miss Meadows took a step back, slipping in the mud, before she turned and fled across the road, shouting back to them, "Someone intends to blow up Hampton Court Palace."

# CHAPTER 3

"Say that again." Francis Walsingham leaned forward from behind his desk, glowering at Kit and Iomhar. His greying brows were so furrowed that they looked rather like thin mice that had crawled onto his forehead and died there, with their chins tucked under.

"Ye heard us right, Walsingham," Iomhar replied first as he sat on the windowsill, glancing out at Seething Lane. "That was what Miss Meadows said."

"Kit." Walsingham's voice was so sharp that she jutted her chin higher, standing in the middle of the floor like she had in her childhood, when she'd been called to this room because she'd been misbehaving or had not been working hard enough. "Tell me you did not help this woman out of Nottingham Castle." His black eyes pierced her to the core.

"I'd best keep my lips closed." Kit's words were enough to make him strike the table with both fists. He clearly regretted it, wincing at the pain and sitting back so far that Kit wasn't sure if it was his old bones that clicked, or the wood of the chair.

"You were instructed to retrieve the message from Miss Meadows. Nothing more."

"She would not utter the message unless I helped her beyond the castle's walls." Kit held her ground, crossing her arms over her chest. "They will find her again soon enough. She did not strike me as the boldest of people. She will not do well on the run."

"Have ye not already sent men searching for her?" Iomhar asked, taking up the thread of the conversation.

Walsingham flicked his eyes toward Iomhar. "You take delight in defending Kit these days, do you not?"

"I am asking a question. That is all." Iomhar leaned forward, resting his elbows on his knees and not looking up to meet Kit's curious eyes.

"You defend her a lot." Walsingham's words made Kit shift from one foot to the other, uncomfortable at the implication.

"We work together," Iomhar said carefully. "That means her mistakes are mine, as well as hers."

"It was not a mistake," Kit insisted. Iomhar flicked his gaze to her. It was brief, but she knew it was a warning look, telling her to be quiet. She decided not to adhere. "Did it not work?" she asked, looking between Iomhar and Walsingham.

Iomhar accepted it with a slow nod, sitting back again, but Walsingham did not. He slowly rose to his feet, lifting a curling hand to his aching back as he bent over the desk.

"You do not know if it worked. Miss Meadows could have told you any lies, anything at all to obtain her freedom. Gold-plated lies!"

"You do not believe it, then?" Kit asked, tilting her head as she watched Walsingham closely. "You think it was a creation? A lie that someone intends to blow up the palace?"

"It is too secure for such a wild thing to be possible," Walsingham said dismissively, sweeping papers across his desk as he came to stand in front of Kit. "No place is more closely guarded in this country."

"Except the Tower," said Iomhar, earning a glare from Walsingham. "Ye wish me to be silent?"

"Yes, I do. Keep your mouth closed whilst I'm telling Kit what an error she has made."

Kit bristled at the words. She tried to stand taller, but the anger in Walsingham's small eyes made her spine involuntarily slouch.

"She did not make an error."

"I said be quiet, Iomhar," Walsingham warned.

Iomhar just shrugged, his mind clearly made up. "Aye, she still obtained the message."

"He is allowed to agree with me once in a while," said Kit, unwilling to let Walsingham continue to look between them with what appeared to be suspicion.

"Aye, must be a blue moon tonight," Iomhar said, looking out of the window and up into the fair sky above.

"Why do you not believe it is possible? This plot?" Kit asked Walsingham. "Miss Meadows sounded sincere."

"You cannot be sure of that. Some people are just good liars."

"Agreed, but if she was going to make up some lie, why would it be this one?" Kit shook her head in disbelief.

"Because it is dramatic, is it not? It sounds like the plot of one of those silly theatre plays. Who would try to put gunpowder in a place as secure as Hampton Court Palace? The challenge would be immense."

"That is why they would do it," Kit said quietly, as a thought clicked into place. "Because no one would ever suspect it possible."

Her words seemed to strike Walsingham like an arrow to his stomach. He inched back, the heels of his shoes clicking on the wood as he clasped his hands over his gut.

"No, I do not believe it." Despite his words, his face paled.

"You do believe it." Kit was insistent. "You just do not *wish* to believe it."

Walsingham kept moving backward until he collided with the desk behind him, scattering papers from the surface. Silence stretched between them, with neither Kit nor Walsingham breaking their stare. Eventually, Kit shifted awkwardly. She was too much reminded of a day during her youth when she was supposed to be studying her codes in the attic. When Walsingham had discovered she had crept out through the attic window and spent most of the afternoon traversing rooftops, he'd been livid, and had called her to this room. "Some intelligencer you will make, Kitty," he had scoffed.

"It should be impossible." Walsingham broke the silence, calling Kit's thoughts back to the present. "No one could sneak barrels of gunpowder into a palace."

"Nay one said it would be in barrels," said Iomhar. He was looking out of the window once again, scratching his chin. "We wouldn't use barrels, would we? We'd be more inventive than that."

"By God's blood!" Walsingham cursed, hurrying behind the desk to his seat. Kit and Iomhar exchanged a look as he dropped into the creaking chair. It was something Kit rather suspected Walsingham depended on, as if this position gave him power. His only weapons were the paper and quill before him.

"Do you believe it possible now?" Kit asked, warily watching as Walsingham rubbed his hands across his cheeks, his distress evident.

"She is already… The queen, she is…"

"Already what?" Kit asked.

"She is already dying, Kit." Walsingham's words made Kit move forward quickly. She reached the other side of the desk and stared down at him.

"Dying?" she asked, startled by the tightening of her chest. It was as if something was withering inside of her. "You said the queen was sick, that physicians were with her night and day. She was well cared for — these were your words."

"I will say nearly anything to keep the peace," Walsingham said quietly, lowering his hands from his cheeks. "She is sick indeed. I feel like I am turning back the moons, back to sixty-two again."

"What happened then? In sixty-two?" Iomhar asked from his place at the window.

"Smallpox," Walsingham said darkly. "I stood outside our queen's chamber and prayed as I have never prayed before. I feel as if those nights are upon us now."

"She is dying," Kit murmured, moving away. She didn't really know where her feet were taking her, but she found herself heading toward where Iomhar sat in the window. "Miss Meadows said the men she overhead knew that the queen was sick."

"She did," Iomhar agreed with a nod.

"So why not leave it at that? Why not leave the queen to die if they already know of her sickness?"

"They must want to be certain of that death." Iomhar spoke slowly, meeting her gaze. "They don't want to leave her death to the wee chances."

"Or maybe…" Kit whispered, another thought coming into focus.

"What?" Iomhar sat taller.

"Or maybe they want her to die in a horrible way."

"God have mercy, Kit! Are you done?" Walsingham exclaimed from the desk.

"It has to be said." Kit sighed, reluctant to look round and meet Walsingham's eyes.

"Aye, I agree." Iomhar pushed off from the windowsill. "How many men have we seen who would wish for the queen to die? They want it to be horrific, to be the ones to claim victory for their side."

"You are both sickening me," Walsingham said miserably, holding his head in his hands.

"Ye are right," Iomhar whispered, so quietly that only Kit could hear him. "I can imagine many who would think in such a way."

She knew exactly who he was referring to. "Including…?"

"Aye, including him," Iomhar nodded.

"Enough of this." Walsingham's voice urged them both to look away from each other and turn to face him. "I do not want to believe it, but we must face the possibility." He dragged forward a piece of parchment and scribbled an order upon it. "The council must be informed, and a search of Hampton Court must be conducted. This day, this afternoon."

"Ye'll need many men to do the search fast enough."

"Then you will join them. Take this with you to the palace." He blew on the ink before folding up the parchment, leaving an imprint on the other side. Clearly, they had no time to wait for the ink to dry properly. He secured the letter with red wax, pressing his seal into it. "Go, take it now. I will follow behind and instruct the search. You can begin. This will give you the authority at the palace."

Iomhar took the letter and went to leave the room with Kit following behind.

"Not you, Kit."

Kit froze, as did Iomhar. He was the first to turn round, looking at Kit with raised eyebrows.

"But you send us on every commission together," said Kit, glancing over her shoulder.

"Not today."

"Why not?" Iomhar asked, his voice strangely sharp, prompting Kit to look toward him with a frown.

"I do not have to explain myself." Walsingham gestured between them with his quill. "Iomhar, go now to the palace. Kit, back here."

"One second." Iomhar moved to Kit's side and whispered in her ear. "Ye need to talk to him."

"What are you two whispering about?" Walsingham called.

"Must the spymaster know all?" Iomhar asked, raising his voice again.

"Sometimes I think you do not really understand what I do here, Iomhar," Walsingham said, clasping his hands in front of him.

"Ask him if it is a memory or not," Iomhar urged Kit.

She felt the strength leave her body. Back in Northumberland, before Yuletide, she had told Iomhar of the dream she kept having, in which she was trapped underwater with Walsingham reaching down to pull her out.

"It is not the time," she whispered back, aware of how close Iomhar had come to speak in her ear.

His expression softened. "Aye, there will never be a right time, but ye still need to ask."

"I am growing impatient, Kit," Walsingham called from the other side of the room.

"Go," Kit said a little louder to Iomhar, widening her eyes.

He nodded, glancing back once from the doorway. As his footsteps retreated down the staircase, making the boards creak and echo through the house, Kit faced Walsingham.

"Sit, Kit." He beckoned her closer, to where a chair was placed on the other side of the desk. She sat down, uncomfortable in the Savonarola chair with its crossed legs and wide back.

"I know you think I made a mistake. You do not need to tell me as much again."

"That is not what I wish to say." Walsingham sat back, his body limp, as if the will to fight and be angry had fled from him. As he tipped his chin upwards, resting the back of his neck on the curve of his seat, light from the window bathed his gaunt features. It struck Kit how old he was beginning to look, the shape of his skull more and more prominent through his skin these days. "Iomhar is right. They will pick up Miss Meadows again soon enough. Either way, she is no great threat. A minor noblewoman with letters sent to the King of France that went unanswered. She had no more effect than a fly does to parchment."

"Then what is it you wish to say?" Kit asked, aware as she spoke that Walsingham was peering at her.

"What happened to you, Kit?"

"What do you mean?" she asked, sitting a little further forward.

"When I first placed you with Iomhar, you detested the idea of working with anyone else. Now you look to each other for confirmation of everything." Walsingham splayed his hands. "Neither of you can think without the other's say so."

"We work well together." Kit shrugged, wanting to believe it was no wondrous thing. "I may say this little, but you were right. It was perhaps wise to put us together."

"Was it?" Walsingham's words were rather eager as he leaned forward. "You are close. Too close. Could you work alone? If I asked it of you?"

"Easily," Kit answered.

"There is nothing else I should know, is there?"

"In what way?"

Walsingham tilted his head, eyeing her as an owl would a mouse in a field. "The partnership. It remains a professional one, does it not?"

"I beg your pardon?" Kit wasn't aware of jumping to her feet, but she suddenly found herself standing before Walsingham.

"You heard me, Kit."

"Of course it is professional."

"You share jests. You whisper together in front of my own eyes. In Northumberland, he wrote to me, pleading for you to be allowed to come home because someone was hunting you."

"That was the act of a friend," Kit insisted. "He was trying to save my life."

"He was not putting your life above every other priority, then?" Walsingham asked.

Kit's lips parted and closed, desperately seeking an answer that wouldn't come. There was a loud rap at the door.

"Not now!" Walsingham snapped.

"It cannot wait," a man called from the other side of the door.

"Beale? What do you want?" Walsingham demanded, recognising the voice. The door opened and Robert Beale ran in, giving Kit the freedom to turn away. Beale was now much recovered from his time trapped in the fire in Seething Lane the summer before, yet he coughed as he moved. Kit rather suspected the cough would stay with him for good.

She tried to straighten her clothes, hoping that the simple action would help align her thoughts, before she turned back to face the two men. Beale was forcing a letter into Walsingham's hands.

"From Lord Burghley," he said impatiently. "An apothecary has been with the queen this morning. He had something to say."

Walsingham wasted no time in tearing open the red wax seal. His eyes hopped along the words before his lips flattened into a line. His face had paled so much that Kit knew straight away that something was wrong.

"It is the queen, her sickness…" He paused, swallowing. "It is not a natural sickness at all."

"What is it then?" Kit asked, going very still.

"She has been poisoned."

# CHAPTER 4

"Be prepared, Kit, it is not a fine sight," Walsingham whispered as Kit was led through the corridors of Hampton Court. In the fading evening light, the hallways looked darker to her than she remembered, with barely any candles lit. Kit could see through the window to the base courtyard where people usually gathered, waiting for an audience with the queen. Today, the only people wandering the cobbles were gentlemen-at-arms, searching every crevice and shadow.

"Have you heard from Iomhar?" Kit asked Walsingham.

He turned, glaring at her. "Are you asking for news of him to see whether he has found the gunpowder, or for another reason?" His words made something jolt inside of her.

"Do not doubt my focus, Walsingham," she said darkly.

They walked on in silence, passing at the end of the corridor through a set of double doors carved with vines and fruit. Beyond the doors a gentleman-at-arms stood, carrying a rapier in his belt. With one nod from Walsingham, he moved to the side, allowing them to pass.

Trailing up a thin set of steps, Kit looked back and forth, realising she had not climbed them before. This part of the palace creaked more than the other, suggesting it was older. Even the walls were more closed in, the darkness more oppressive, save for one candle that was placed at the top of the stairs.

"Where are we?" Kit asked, her voice quiet.

"We are not going to have an *audience* with the queen, Kit. Nothing so formal," Walsingham said over his shoulder as he led the way up the stairs. "We are to see the queen as few people see her." When he reached the top, he turned, gesturing down at her clothes with his long bony fingers. "I should have asked you to change first."

"Why?" Kit asked. "I am not standing on ceremony."

"Perhaps not. Straighten your clothes, at least." He walked on, leaving Kit to glance down at the doublet she was wearing, retying some of the laces that had come loose across her chest and hiding her white linen shirt beneath. Reaching for her cap, she tucked her short red locks deeper beneath the material, trying to hide the wildness caused by the wind.

They crossed into a new corridor, this one guarded by not only two gentlemen-at-arms, but also a lady, who was so short in stature that Kit almost missed her. She nodded to the two of them as they came toward her.

"How does she fare, my lady?" Walsingham asked, adopting a much more formal tone. Kit eyed him carefully, noticing how he was changing before her. Gone was the spymaster of business; he was standing a little taller now, becoming the secretary of the Privy Council.

"Wait for your eyes to tell you," the lady said with a shake of her head. "Words do not do the matter justice."

Walsingham nodded. Beckoning Kit to follow, he passed the lady-in-waiting and hurried down the corridor. At the end of the hallway, three men were gathered outside of the bedchamber door. Lord Burghley was amongst them, his eyes wide like an owl's as he turned toward Walsingham.

"You received my message?" Lord Burghley asked, not bothering with pleasantries.

"I did."

"Who is this?" Lord Burghley asked, gesturing in Kit's direction with his cane. "We need more than just a boy to guard her."

"That is not a boy," Walsingham answered before Kit could. She lifted her chin a little higher, revealing her face beneath the brim of her hat. Lord Burghley leaned abruptly forward, as if in disbelief. "Kit comes with me."

"Very well. The apothecary is inside. We were waiting for you to tell the queen."

"Then lead on." Walsingham's voice turned graver as Lord Burghley entered through the door, glancing back at Kit with his brows furrowed.

"Walsingham?" Kit followed him into the room. "Why am I here?"

"Wait, Kit. You will see shortly." Walsingham urged her to step away with an impatient flick of his hand.

Beyond the door was a series of private chambers. The air was filled with herbal scents, and Kit had to wrinkle her nose to stop herself from sneezing.

"Rosemary..." she whispered, recognising the smells in turn. "Camomile." She had met such scents before, in Walsingham's kitchen when his housekeeper, Doris, had been cooking. Lord Burghley and Walsingham moved to another gentleman's side, a tall and lanky fellow who stood in the very middle of the first room, the privy chamber. Kit followed the trail of the herbs, finding bundles hung down from above doorways. Sorrel was there too, with leathery dark green leaves starting to turn a reddish brown, like blood dripping from the timbers. Kit recognised most of the herbs, apart from one. In the middle of one of the herbs was a purple flower, consisting of small spikes. She eyed the plant for some time, certain she had seen it somewhere before, though she could not think where.

"You are certain of this?" Walsingham asked, his tone so harsh that Lord Burghley lifted his hands in a calming gesture.

"Shh," he said and used his cane to point through the open doorway to the withdrawing chamber. Kit could see ladies hurrying back and forth, some urging for fresh water and sheets to be brought, others with their noses in handkerchiefs. On the other side was a second doorway, across which was a thin net, practically shimmering thanks to the number of candles that were beyond.

"Tell me again," Walsingham urged the lanky apothecary. "Her humours are imbalanced?"

"Yes, I am sure of it. Sanguine. She is too hot, and she sweats, her temple constantly moist."

"And the cause?"

"Poison."

"Yes, but what poison?"

"I do not know." The apothecary shook his head vigorously, looking as if he feared for his life. Kit moved back to Walsingham's side, watching as he began to fidget more and more.

"Then find out, Morgan," Walsingham ordered. Morgan chose not to respond; he only hung his head a little.

"Do we know what was poisoned?" Kit asked. "How she ingested it?"

Lord Burghley turned slowly toward her, his lip curling in surprise, as if he had not expected her to be capable of speech at all. "We are asking the questions," he said tightly. Kit did not miss the reproach, but she refused to back away.

"It is a good question," Walsingham said, turning back to the apothecary. "Do you have an answer?"

"No." Morgan spoke slowly. "All her food was tested as normal."

The netting across the doorway to the other room was brushed aside suddenly. The scents of more herbs filled the air, this time coupled with a sweetness and the unmistakeable fragrance of mint. A plump lady-in-waiting moved into the withdrawing chamber.

"She knows you are here," she said calmly. "If you are to speak of her, she asks that she is included in the conversation."

"I did not ask…" a rather weak voice protested from the bedchamber. "I ordered."

Lord Burghley walked forward first, followed by Walsingham, who took Kit's arm and pulled her after him. In the bedchamber, Kit thought all had turned a murky shade of yellow. With so many candles lit, it was painful to look around. The windows had been covered with red drapes, and on tables nearby liquids were gathered, most a pale golden colour with dried wormwood sprigs placed beside the cups, and a sugar block that had had grains chipped away.

"Walsingham?" The queen's voice came from the bed.

She was prostrate with her body fully covered by sheets. Her light red hair was thin and splayed across the pillows. Her lips were dry, and her cheeks barely moved, each one the colour of the moon with the same pitted surface. She gripped the sheets as she tried to sit up.

Two ladies-in-waiting hurried forward, including the one that had pushed back the netting. They lifted the queen into a seated position, from where her eyes could find Walsingham and the others.

"You have come to tell me something," she said, her voice rather like that of a child's.

"Your Majesty, it is not that we are —"

"Oh, Burghley." She lifted a feeble hand, and this was enough to quieten him. "Do not treat me as you would your wife's pup. I am no fool just because I am unwell. I can hear my physicians and the apothecary muttering together. My ladies-in-waiting look between each other, their eyes saying much when their lips cannot. As for Mr Dee, well, he refuses to read to me what the stars say of my life at this moment. Is this not enough to know something is amiss?"

Kit chewed the side of her mouth to stop herself from smiling in admiration. Though the queen was sick, she would never allow herself to be seen as the weakest person in the room.

"Walsingham, you must tell me. You are better at speaking of ill news."

Walsingham did not hesitate and stepped nearer to the bed. "The apothecary has found evidence of poison." Despite his quiet voice, it was enough to cause a commotion.

The ladies-in-waiting began to mutter, with one even dropping the cup of golden liquid that was in her hands, knocking the mixture everywhere.

"How?" the queen asked.

"They do not know. Neither do we know what the poison is. Yet."

The queen nodded slowly, before turning her eyes up to the plump lady beside her. Kit watched the queen's face carefully. She was attempting to stay stoic, as if unmoved by the situation, but her acting talents only went so far. Her lips quivered for a second before she pressed them together.

"Will I live?" the queen asked.

Lord Burghley was the one to step forward this time. "You are fighting it, Your Majesty. Yet you must continue to fight it."

"Do you think I lie here doing nothing?" she asked, attempting to laugh. The sound was hollow. "Every grain of energy in my body goes into lifting my hands or blinking. Do not tell me to fight, Burghley. I know very well what I am doing."

"We must step up the protection for the queen," Lord Burghley insisted, turning to face Walsingham.

"I know," he responded calmly.

"You already have gentlemen-at-arms watching my every move beyond these walls," the queen said, gesturing to the door of her bedchamber. "I will not have them watching me in here too."

"With respect, Your Majesty, your ladies-in-waiting are not enough protection," Lord Burghley whispered, clasping his cane tighter.

The queen did not argue with him, but neither did she concede he was right. "I will not have a man in this room watching me sleep." She held his gaze as she spoke.

"You will not have to," Walsingham said, speaking up before Lord Burghley could utter another word. "Your Majesty, you have met before, but may I reintroduce you to one of my intelligencers? You last met in the Thames." Walsingham stepped back and to the side, revealing where Kit was standing.

The queen's lips flickered into the smallest of smiles. "The woman who dresses as a man," she said with a small trace of humour. "I remember you. You pulled me from the Thames. You made rather a mess of one of my finest dresses, I seem to remember, but ... I could not have swum out of there alone." She nodded at Kit, as if in thanks. "Remind me of your name."

"Kit, Your Majesty." Kit did her best not to fidget, though the collective gaze of the room was enough to make her sweat. "Kit Scarlett."

"Is that your real name?"

Kit looked to Walsingham, unsure of how to answer the question.

"It is the name I gave to her." Walsingham's words were enough to quieten the matter. "I think it best we assign Kit to guard you, Your Majesty. For now."

"Very well." The queen looked away. "Though I hope you are fond of conversation, Kit. My ladies do that more than anything else." The ladies all smiled. "Well? Is there anything else?"

"No, Your Majesty. We will leave you to sleep." Lord Burghley gestured to the door with his cane, urging Walsingham to step through. He motioned to Kit too, demanding that she followed.

The net was dropped behind them as they moved into the withdrawing chamber and then straight into the privy chamber, where the door to the corridor was opened by one of the gentlemen-at-arms.

"Guard her as if it is your own life you are protecting," Lord Burghley ordered Kit.

"I'll guard her better than that, my lord." Her words seemed to surprise him, making one brow curve before he looked to Walsingham.

"Do you have no better?"

"We will increase the protection on the castle, but Kit is the best person to stay with the queen. Trust me, Lord Burghley."

"You trust her, it seems. That will have to be enough," Lord Burghley said with a sigh.

Kit turned to Walsingham, startled by the confidence he had in her. He appeared to be avoiding her gaze.

"Kit, everyone who tries to see the queen, you prevent. The only people allowed in that room are the two of us, the physicians, the apothecary, Mr John Dee, and her ladies. Yes?" Lord Burghley asked impatiently.

"Yes, my lord," Kit nodded.

"Good. Now, Walsingham, would you care to explain to me why we have ordered a search of the palace?"

Walsingham was evidently trying to keep his nerves hidden as he scratched his cheek. "There is something you must know."

"Walsingham?" someone called from down the corridor. Recognising the voice, Kit turned with a smile to see it was Iomhar approaching. The moment he saw her there, he returned the smile.

"What, Iomhar? Has the search been done?"

"Nay, we have only begun, but not all of the gentlemen-at-arms will help and refuse to let us pass."

"What?" Walsingham turned to Burghley. "I gave Iomhar the authority to conduct a search."

"I will not let any man search these corridors, least of all a Scot I do not know." Lord Burghley's words made Iomhar stiffen, his hands resting on his weapons belt. Kit tried to keep the smile off her face, remembering what had happened to the last man who had insulted Iomhar because of where he came from.

"You will authorise that search," Walsingham declared, stepping toward Burghley.

"Why?"

"Because the palace could be burnt down around us if you do not." Walsingham's statement made Burghley freeze. "Iomhar, come with me. I will get you past the protection." He beckoned Iomhar to follow, but he didn't straight away. He turned to Kit instead.

"Did ye speak to him?" he whispered.

"Not yet."

"Why are ye here?"

"It seems I have a new commission." She glanced at the queen's door, enough of an answer.

"Then stay safe," Iomhar warned. "Men will do many a thing to get past this door."

"Iomhar!" Walsingham barked from down the corridor. "Enough whispering."

"Aye, I'm coming," Iomhar called, looking at Kit one last time. "Shout if ye need help." He winked at her before he hurried after Walsingham. Kit tried not to think of what the wink meant, nor did she dwell on why it had made her smile so much. Instead, she turned her gaze on Lord Burghley, who had not moved since Walsingham had mentioned burning.

"Are you well, my lord?" she asked.

"Guard her," he urged. "Even if it kills you to do it."

"You have my word," she promised before backing into the chamber, closing the door firmly on Lord Burghley's quivering face.

# CHAPTER 5

"The queen has eaten nothing different at all?" Kit asked, looking around at the ladies-in-waiting that had gathered at her side. They all shook their heads in unison.

"Not a thing." The plump lady spoke quickly. It was she who had encouraged them into the bedchamber earlier that day to meet the queen. "We eat the same, and the queen has her own taster. He is perfectly well."

Kit scrunched her brow, for it made little sense. If the queen had consumed the same food and drinks as her ladies and her taster, how was she the only one to fall sick? It suggested the poison had found another way into her system.

"What do we call you?" one of the older ladies asked Kit, looking at her clothes with curiosity.

"My name is Kit Scarlett. You can call me Kit," she said, watching in surprise as the lady touched the sleeve of her doublet.

"How can you wear these things?" she asked in amazement. "My father would never have allowed such a thing when I was your age! It is quite remarkable."

"No father would," the plump lady-in-waiting said, turning her eyes away from Kit, as if she could not bear the sight of such male clothes upon a woman.

"Well, I suppose one must have a father around to offer such opinions to begin with." Kit's tart reply did little to soften the harsh expression of the rotund lady, yet the woman at her side offered a sad smile. "What are your names?"

"I am Miss Parry," said the older woman beside her. She had large eyes and very curved eyebrows, like two perfect crescent moons. Her whitening hair was tucked under her muslin cap. "I am the keeper of the jewellery box."

"Does it need keeping?" Kit asked in amusement.

"Of course it does," the plump lady answered before Miss Parry had time. "I am Lady Hunsdon." She stood a little taller with the words, showing off the full extent of her broad figure. There were small dimples in her cheeks, as if they had been pecked out by a bird with a sharp beak, and her nose was misaligned, practically crooked, leading Kit to suspect that it may have once been broken. "I am the lady of the privy chamber."

"It means she approves who enters these chambers," said a young lady on Kit's other side. She had dark hair, equally dark eyes and a swanlike neck, so long it almost looked unnatural. "I am Lady Gifford, one of the queen's maids of honour." She began to gesture across the room. "That there is Lady Stafford." She motioned to one of the older ones in the group, who sat hunched with her lips firmly pressed together, as if uttering words of any kind was a challenge to her.

"She is one of the queen's most loyal friends," Lady Hunsdon spoke up, smiling for the first time. "Then there is Miss Wyngfield, Miss Radcliff, and Lady Howard." She pointed toward three ladies that were gathered together, all busy preparing some new sheets to be placed upon the queen's bed. "Then, of course, there is Lady Hardwick." Lady Hunsdon's voice became strained as she pointed toward the tall lady at the far side of the room.

Lady Hardwick had greying ginger hair and eyebrows that were barely discernible. Her green eyes darted across the younger ladies, almost calculating as she drew them into conversation, professing to know a tale about some courtier that would make them gasp. Kit was trying to remember where she had heard the name Lady Hardwick before, when her focus was taken by the conversation. She was startled that the ladies were at all interested in gossiping at a time like this.

"They seem intent on conversation." Kit spoke slowly, folding her arms across her chest.

"That is the way ladies of the chamber are," Miss Parry said with a soft laugh, as if it were all some sort of game. At a harsh look from Lady Hunsdon, Miss Parry's laughter died as she glanced at the net curtain across the door.

"It helps to cheer one's spirits when we need relief from the darkness." Lady Gifford's voice intimated courage as Kit turned her eyes on her. She could see she was not so afraid of Lady Hunsdon's ill opinion. "So, we are to have the pleasure of your company, Miss Scarlett?"

"I will be here, certainly." Kit spoke lightly. She was not sure she would describe the meeting as a pleasure. Her eyes would not stop dancing across the ladies as more and more of them were drawn into the gossip. "Please, call me Kit."

"I think it best we hold onto formalities." Lady Hunsdon's voice brooked no refusal. Her dark blue eyes were turned in Kit's direction and the jewels in her hair glittered in the light. "You will be Miss Scarlett in these chambers. All ladies in here are addressed using their title."

"Yes, Lady Hunsdon, but Miss Scarlett is perhaps not one for the formalities, is she?" Miss Parry said with a giggle, though once again that laugh quickly faded. Kit decided she rather liked Miss Parry's way of handling the matter and nodded to her in agreement, but Lady Hunsdon was clearly not so keen. "Where did you get your clothes?" Miss Parry asked, stepping closer to Kit. Before Kit could answer, a hand closed around Miss Parry's arm. Lady Hunsdon was stopping her from saying any more.

"That is enough for now. We will leave Miss Scarlett to her task, as she will leave us to ours."

With that, Kit was dismissed to the corner of the room, feeling as if she was blending in with the many faces upon the tapestry. More than once, Lady Hunsdon caught the ladies staring at her and flicked her fingers at them. At one point, Kit heard her muttering a warning to one of the younger ladies.

"It does not do well to stare at those ladies who are not quite as they should be."

Kit stifled her smile. She was quite happy to be different from the ladies in that room.

Kit sprinted up the stairs toward her attic room. She didn't have long. The cart was still waiting for her outside, preparing to take her back to Hampton Court. She just had long enough to collect some clothes and a few things before she would have to head back.

In the fading evening light, the orange glow through the window was mixed with shadows, making the steps difficult to see. She trampled up them by memory until she reached the ledge outside her door, tripping on the top step as she saw that something was bathed in the evening light.

The door to her room was slightly ajar.

Placing her fingers on the handle, she bent her head down. The wood had been chipped away from around the lock.

"By blood," she murmured, wincing as she remembered just how many times Iomhar had warned her that the door was easy to get past.

Casting her gaze around the empty stairwell one last time, Kit placed a hand on one of the hilts of the daggers in her belt before flinging the door open.

"Who is there?" she cried, running inside. The shadows were long, but the light streaming through the two loft windows was enough for her to see the place was empty. "My God…" she murmured, turning her head back and forth as her eyes focused. The room had been ransacked. Clothes from her oak coffer had been thrown to the floor, along with her tallow candlesticks.

Kit didn't hesitate. She ran forward and checked her coffer, collecting the scattered items. Even the bed had been rummaged through, with the sheets pulled off the straw mattress, yet there was nothing missing.

"What did they want?" she murmured to the open air, fearing it was no passing thief who had broken into her room.

When there was a tap on the chamber door in the early hours of the morning, Kit was almost the only person left awake in the queen's rooms. The queen was still sleeping and wheezing, her breath so ragged that more than once Lady Hunsdon leaned toward her with concern. Other ladies, including Lady Gifford and Lady Hardwick, had fallen asleep in odd positions in the withdrawing chamber. Lady Hardwick was still sitting up, her head leaning on the wall beside her with one cheek flattened, whilst Lady Gifford and Miss Radcliff were leaning against each other.

"It is late," Lady Hunsdon said as she looked out the window. "Who would call at this time to see the queen?"

"They might be looking for one of us," Kit answered, getting to her feet. "I will go."

Lady Hunsdon nodded, before turning her focus back to the queen.

"You must sleep sometime, Lady Hunsdon."

She smiled briefly, a trace of humour in her dark eyes. "If you were sat here in my shoes and farthingale, you would not sleep either."

Kit turned away, observing from the corner of her eye the way Lady Hunsdon stood and moved back to the bedchamber, reaching out to the queen with gentle fingers. There was an intimacy there, one Kit had not seen between the queen and another before.

Kit crossed to the main door of the privy chamber, just as whoever was on the other side grew impatient and tapped again.

"Yes?" Kit murmured as she opened the door but a slither. At first, she could see nothing on the other side except darkness, until a candle moved and revealed a face.

"Good evening to ye too, Kit."

"Iomhar?" Kit stepped out of the door and closed it behind her, urging Iomhar to back up a step to make room for her. "What are you doing here at this time of night?"

"What do ye think?" he asked with a smirk as he placed the candle on a ledge in the woodwork nearby and leaned against the wall. "Our search hasn't finished. Nay one seems particularly happy to let intelligencers and soldiers search when they aren't being told what we are searching for."

"Have you found anything?" Kit asked, mirroring his stance.

"Aye, sure we have, that's why we're still searching," he said with sarcasm, earning a tap on the arm from Kit. "Nay in the mood for jesting?"

"The jesting mood has certainly not struck me tonight." Kit sighed. Her mind was on one thing only: the way that the queen was flat out on that bed, barely moving, except for her laboured breaths.

"Ye're afraid," Iomhar murmured, moving an inch nearer.

Kit returned her gaze to him, startled to find him so close. She didn't have the words to explain her anxiety, so she simply shrugged.

Iomhar shook his head slowly. "She has the best physicians with her, doesn't she?"

"They do not have the power of miracles. She needs the hand of God to heal her now."

"Perhaps He is watching over her."

"I see the devil at work in there," Kit whispered, looking over her shoulder, wary of any gentlemen-at-arms walking down the corridor and overhearing.

"What do ye mean?"

"I mean the ladies-in-waiting."

"Since when does the devil go round wearing stays and a farthingale?"

"You never know, it might suit him." Kit's words pulled a small smile to Iomhar's face.

"What are ye not saying, Kit?" His tone was solemn.

"There is something in that room," she mused, her words coming slowly. "Something that is not right. I cannot put my finger on it, but there is a lot that unsettles me." She checked that the door was firmly closed before she went on. "Some of the ladies seem more interested in talking amongst themselves than they are in our queen's health."

"Ye think they do not care for her?"

"I think they care for their position. If she dies, they'll certainly be upset when their position at court disappears." Kit shifted back and forth. "Lady Hunsdon, she is the queen's closest friend, that is easy to see. Lady Gifford and Lady Hardwick are the ones who talk the most. They were telling tales, making one another laugh."

"Perhaps they do not take the matter seriously. If the queen dies, we could see a civil war. Think on it, who would vie for the throne?"

Kit didn't want to answer. She had heard Mary Stuart's name whispered and shouted too much in the last year.

"She will never be Queen of England." At Kit's words, Iomhar's eyebrows quirked up. "You think she will be?"

"I hope she will never be, but the possibility increases if our queen dies. She is the next in line." Iomhar's whisper sent a shiver through Kit's bones. She shifted from foot to foot again, aware that Iomhar had returned his gaze to her.

"You are staring. What is it?"

"I am looking. There is a difference." His smile glimmered through as he bent toward her. "Ye seen anyone? Since we returned from the border?"

"What do you mean?" Kit pretended innocence, earning a glare from Iomhar.

"Do not play games," he warned. "Ye were hunted enough in the north, and there is nothing to say that Lord Ruskin would not send someone after ye here. Just because nothing happened over Yuletide doesn't mean he will not try again now the new year has come."

"It is not so easy to hunt me in the middle of London." Kit looked away.

"Have ye forgotten he and Mary Stuart have supporters everywhere?" Iomhar scoffed. "Don't be a fool, Kit. Lord Ruskin can send men after ye here, just as easily as he did in Northumberland. Have ye seen anything? Anyone following ye? Anyone trailing behind in your shadow?"

"No." Kit shook her head. She didn't think this was the best time to tell him that she was certain someone had been in her rooms. What good would that do? It could have been some passing thief, or a child acting on a dare. It was odd, though, that nothing had been taken.

"Ye are hiding something."

"You do not need to know all my secrets."

"I know a fair few of them by now." He smiled, as if delighted by the idea.

"Do not remind me," she huffed.

"Which brings us to our other point: when are ye going to ask Walsingham about that memory?"

"Not now, Iomhar. He is busy."

"When is a spymaster not busy?"

"When the country is at peace."

"Ye'll be waiting a long time, then."

"So be it," she declared and turned back to the queen's door. "I need to return to my place beside the queen."

"I'll leave ye to it." Iomhar began to walk away but as he inched past her, he bent down and whispered in her ear from behind. "Watch your back, Kit."

She couldn't explain why this sent a shiver down her spine. "Why do I need to do that?" she asked as she hurriedly opened the door.

"Because I am not beside ye to do it for ye." He was too far off for Kit to reply, disappearing down a set of narrow steps as she retreated into the queen's chambers.

## CHAPTER 6

"What are you doing?" Lady Hunsdon's question made Kit slow down, but she didn't stop moving.

"Searching," she answered quietly, tiptoeing around the ladies who were all still sleeping. The morning light streamed into the withdrawing chamber, illuminating all the ladies who had not made it to their beds the previous night. Neither Kit nor Lady Hunsdon had done any better. Kit had managed an hour or so before the sun had risen, so she was yawning every few seconds and stretching her arms. Lady Hunsdon had managed a little longer, with her forehead resting on the mattress as she kneeled beside the queen's bed.

"What are you searching for?" Lady Hunsdon followed Kit around the withdrawing chamber.

"I do not know that until I find it." Kit's words prompted Lady Hunsdon to cross her arms, her chin jerking upwards. "What?"

"You are an odd sort of woman."

"Thank you, I choose to take that as a compliment." Kit bent down, searching the narrow gap beneath a settle bench. She was about to raise herself up when something caught her eye beneath the bed. She reached under, pulling out a single sprig from a tree. "What is this?" she asked, standing again.

"Willow. It's supposed to ward off evils of the mind." Lady Hunsdon snatched the sprig back and bent down, struggling with her farthingale and the skirt of her dress as she returned the twig to its place. "We place it under all the queen's furniture at this moment."

Kit scrunched her nose as she moved away. While the other ladies were all busying themselves with sleeping during the night and talking amongst themselves when they were awake, Lady Hunsdon seemed to have control of this room.

Kit crossed the space, hoping to shed Lady Hunsdon from her shadow. She stopped in front of a vast window. To the side was a screen, beside which was a table of glass vials and small pots, each one full of makeup and ointments. Kit looked up from the table to see Lady Hunsdon was at her side once more, flicking the ruff around her neck a little lower, the better to watch what Kit was doing.

"This is the queen's private affair," she whispered. "No one must see this." She waved at the makeup.

"Except the ladies-in-waiting." Kit lifted a lid on a small copper pot and peered inside to find small white pellets. There was a dish of water beside it, seemingly used to grind down these pellets into a paste. "What is this?"

Lady Hunsdon didn't reply. She took the lid out of Kit's hands and attempted to place it back on the pot, but Kit snatched it away, lifting it to her nose and inhaling the scent. There was something vinegary about it, tangy and metallic.

"This is not for an unnatural woman to see." Lady Hunsdon managed to take the pot back, leaving Kit reeling.

"What did you call me?" she asked, her voice a little louder than before.

"Shh!" Lady Hunsdon urged, hurrying to replace the lid. She gestured down at the clothes Kit was wearing and widened her eyes, as if the matter was plain.

"Because I dress differently, you think me an *unnatural* woman?"

"It is not normal, is it?" Lady Hunsdon asked. "To wish to dress like that."

"I would say painting this on your face is hardly natural either," Kit said with a smile and lifted the pot again, much to Lady Hunsdon's dismay. "Tell me what it is, and I will return it to the table."

"It is Venetian ceruse," Lady Hunsdon said hurriedly, glancing at the door to the bedchamber where the queen was sleeping, clearly fearful of being caught. Yet the queen was too far away to hear them. "Why do you wish to know?"

Kit returned the pot to the table and reached for another. This one was a much smaller pot, gold in colour. When Kit lifted the lid she found a dark red powder beneath, with signs of fingers that had been pushed inside repeatedly over a number of days.

"This is too much to bear." Lady Hunsdon attempted to take it back again, only to nearly knock it out of Kit's hands. They both fumbled for it, but Kit won, lifting it to her nose. This one had a deeper and more fragrant scent but was just as unpleasant. "Why do you insist on going through her possessions? Just because this is a world you do not understand —"

"You are right, I do not understand it," Kit agreed with a nod. "However, I do understand that there are other ways to get poison into one's system, without being fed it." Her words made Lady Hunsdon's hands freeze. The white fingers went so still that it was easy for Kit to brush them aside before returning the pot to the table. "What is it?"

"Cinnabar. For her lips," Lady Hunsdon said, her voice much weaker this time. She glanced frantically back to the other ladies, some of whom were rousing from their slumbers. She inched closer to Kit, almost pushing her into the table with her farthingale. "You believe this is how she was poisoned? By something on this table?"

"It has to be considered," Kit whispered, stepping around the farthingale the way she would step around a pony in the street. She then reached for another pot. "This one?"

"It removes the makeup."

Kit sniffed it to find an even stronger metallic scent.

"It's not possible, surely," Lady Hunsdon was muttering to herself. "*We* are the only ones allowed in this room."

"Not quite. Mr John Dee, the apothecary and the physicians are now permitted too, are they not? As for guarding the room, none of us can be certain that no one accessed the chambers while you were all out." Kit spoke her thoughts aloud.

"No. It cannot be. It must have been in her food. We would not allow her chamber to be so unprotected." Lady Hunsdon took another pot out of Kit's hands before she even had the chance to smell it.

"Then why is her taster not on his deathbed too?"

"Shh!" Lady Hunsdon hissed, making a few of the ladies jump on the other side of the room.

"Take your own advice, Lady Hunsdon," Kit said with a mischievous smile, pressing a finger to her lips as she abandoned the pots and reached for a glass vial.

"That is enough." Lady Hunsdon's eyes darkened all the more.

"What is in this?" Kit asked, tilting the vial up to the light that filtered in through the windows. She had no wish to waste time trying to persuade the lady to like her.

"It is her morning tonic," Lady Hunsdon said, her voice tight. "It is harmless. Nothing but herbs and water to invigorate the system."

Kit pulled out the cork. "Herbs?" she whispered in surprise, lifting the opening of the vial close to her eye so she could peer inside. There were a few loose green leaves, but there was something else too, a sort of white sediment.

"Yes, that is all." Lady Hunsdon tried to take the vial back, but Kit refused to let her take it. She turned her back completely on Lady Hunsdon and hastened toward the window, where it was lighter. "This is impertinence, indeed! Miss Scarlett, you are proving yourself as annoying as a pestilence."

"You can call me Kit." Kit didn't turn back or acknowledge the insult, for she was too busy gazing at the sediment — a white powder that looked as if it hadn't quite dissolved.

"I must insist you leave these things alone."

"Very well." Kit corked the vial again and returned it to the table, trying to seem uninterested in what she had found. "Though I do acknowledge something, Lady Hunsdon."

"What is that?"

"It is very odd indeed that you are unwilling to let me look for ways our queen could have been poisoned." Kit's words made Lady Hunsdon stumble on the floorboards as they hurried back across the room.

"Is something happening?" Lady Gifford murmured as she stood, stretching to shed the last throes of her sleep.

"Miss Scarlett is just nosing into things that do not concern her." Lady Hunsdon's words prompted many of the ladies to turn toward Kit, all glaring with suspicion.

"Have no fear, Lady Hunsdon. I do not like you either," Kit said. This time, the ladies hid behind cupped hands and turned away, pretending they were not laughing. "If you would excuse me."

She shot Lady Hunsdon one last victorious look before moving beyond the door, out into the privy chamber. Tossing off her cap and stuffing it into her pocket, she ran her hands through her hair, knowing that something was amiss with that vial. But she couldn't alert the ladies-in-waiting, just in case one of them had placed it there.

Once the physicians arrived with the apothecary to attend the queen, Kit ushered them in — all except Morgan, who had been the one to spot the poison. She grabbed him by the arm to stop him following the others.

"You need to look at something."

"I beg your pardon?" Morgan asked, clearly recognising her urgency enough to lower his voice.

"You cannot tell the physicians, nor the ladies. Anyone."

"Walsingham?"

"Yes, you can tell him," Kit said hurriedly. "There is a vial on the queen's table where she keeps her makeup pots. It is supposedly a concoction of herbs and water, with a small brown cork in the top, yet there is a white sediment at the bottom."

The apothecary's head jerked upwards. "I will retrieve it and see if I can detect what the sediment is."

"Thank you." Kit released him at last, watching as he hurried after the others. She turned in a frantic circle, pulling at her hair as the realisation dawned: someone had poisoned the queen from within the palace walls.

# CHAPTER 7

"What do you mean Walsingham is not here?" Kit asked the gentleman-at-arms that had appeared at the queen's door. He had nothing more to add and merely shrugged. Kit pinched the bridge of her nose. This was not the time for Walsingham to disappear. "Guard this door carefully and do not move."

"Where are you going?" he asked, taking her place outside the chamber door whilst the physicians were with the queen.

"I will return soon." She tossed the words over her shoulder and hurried off. She had to speak to someone about what she had found, what she now suspected, and if Walsingham wasn't here, then there was potentially someone still within the palace's walls whom she did trust with the truth.

She hastened through the palace, nearly losing track of her whereabouts more than once thanks to the labyrinth of panelled corridors and red brick archways. When she found herself in the fountain courtyard, she caught sight of someone she recognised. He also worked for Walsingham and his face was round and pink, rather like the ruddy sheen of an apple.

"How fares the search?" she asked, hurrying toward him.

He stopped pacing and shook his head. "We have searched everywhere, yet nothing has been found. Burghley has asked us to end the search."

"No, no, we cannot do that," Kit argued. If the poison failed to kill the queen, then whoever was behind it would want another way to be rid of her — and gunpowder would certainly fulfil their requirements. "Where is Iomhar?"

"You will find him in the Privy Garden."

"Thank you." Kit hurried off.

"Wait? Is something wrong?"

She didn't answer him; she didn't have time for that, nor the inclination. The fewer people who knew about the vial, the better for now. She didn't want whoever had put the sediment in there to suspect that their actions were being discovered.

Leaving the palace far behind, she passed under an archway and into the garden, turning her head back and forth. The coldness of the winter morning made her bury her fingers deeper into her doublet sleeves as her breath filled the air with small clouds.

"Iomhar?" she called down the garden, but it was too vast and long for such a call to be heard so easily. Turning her back on the knot garden and lawns, she hastened through a long avenue, hurrying into the Privy Garden. Either side, the soil was raked back and dappled with white frost, with barely any signs of greenery peeping through. Even the pebbled ground beneath her feet was frozen, with patches of ice that made her slip every now and then.

She was not sure how long it took her to reach the bottom of the garden, but by the time she was there, the cold was setting into her bones. She grabbed the hat from the pocket in her trousers, pulling it down over her ears to keep out the cold.

"Iomhar?" she called again, twisting her head to look across the box hedges toward where the Thames met the very edge of the gardens.

Twigs snapped nearby, followed by a scuffle in the pebbles. Thinking it had to be Iomhar, she crossed behind box hedges, moving toward the sound. She rounded an evergreen tree just as a figure appeared in the distance. He was too far away for her to possibly see his face, but the large hat was plain, something Iomhar never wore, and the cloak upon his shoulders was wide, making his figure stretch outwards.

"Who's there?" Kit called, expecting a gardener to remove his hand from the cloak and wave to her. Yet the hat was too fine to belong to a garden labourer, and there were no such implements scattered around him. Kit inched forward, feeling her suspicion grow. "Who are you?"

"I have come to see the queen," the voice called back. There was something to the tone she didn't like, something almost recognisable.

"The palace is closed to the queen's guests." Kit's words made the man back up a step, half disappearing behind another box hedge. Walsingham and Burghley had made the decision to close the palace gates the day before, so, if the man wasn't staff, who was he?

"I am an exception. I can assure you that all is perfectly well."

"Then come closer, so I can see your face," Kit ordered. Clearly, the man did not like the idea, for he backed away instantly, colliding with a box hedge and casting red yew berries to the ground as he turned on his heel. "Stop!" Kit yelled.

Yet the stranger did not listen. He fled so fast that the cloak whipped behind him, the black silk rippling. Kit raced after him, leaping past box hedges and slipping on the dewy grass in her effort to keep up.

"What honest man runs?" she whispered into the air, heaving hard.

As the stranger took off down another avenue of bushes, Kit tried to cut the corner. She leapt over a smaller hedge, sprinted across a lawn and then jumped over a flowerbed.

"Iomhar?" she bellowed again.

"Kit?" At last, a voice replied to her from some distant place in the garden.

"Intruder!"

She didn't need to say any more; she could hear him running to her position. She kept her focus on the stranger ahead. Now she was closer to him, she could see that the cloak was surprisingly fine and the hat was pulled low. It was clear he was trying to hide his face.

"Stop!" Kit called, trying to grab the back of the cloak as he ran round a fountain, narrowly missing her grasp. She felt the silk whip past her fingers.

The figure was leaping toward a wall that bordered the end of the garden behind the fountain. He jumped, latching his fingers over the flattened ridge at the top, just as Kit caught up to him. Grabbing hold of the black cloak, she tugged hard, trying to pull him back down to the ground. He lashed out with his foot, attempting to drive his heeled boot into the centre of her chest. She barely missed being struck, diving down and releasing her hold on the cloak.

It was enough for the intruder to launch one leg over the wall, inching closer to his escape. Kit reached another time, taking hold of the cloak and holding him in position, narrowly stopping him from escaping as he swung his second leg over the top of the wall.

Kit pulled at the cloak, yet the stranger was evidently strong and fought against her hold. His body dropped to the other side of the wall as she clung to the edges of the cloak, stopping him from escaping, but also masking his face from her view.

"You will go no further!" Kit cried, tugging on the cloak again. There was an almighty yell from the other side of the wall, as if the figure was in pain, then Kit heard the rip of material. She hauled at the cloak as the tearing continued. It quickly became apparent the body that anchored the cloak was no longer attached to it, for as Kit pulled, the material came away too easily, and she was forced to scamper backward.

"Kit?" Iomhar was calling for her again, but she didn't answer.

She fell backwards, her feet tipping over the edge of the fountain — for a second, she hovered there, one arm waving madly to try and keep her balance as the other clung to the loose cloak. Then she tipped, landing in the shallow water on her rear.

"Kit?" Iomhar's voice was much closer and sounded amused.

She blinked the water away from her eyelashes and peered up to see Iomhar running toward the fountain. When his eyes found hers, his pace slowed, and a smile crept onto his face.

"Say nothing," Kit warned, looking over her shoulder at the fountain. It consisted of a great stone orb with lions' mouths on either side, from which streams of water poured. One of these streams was landing on Kit's neck and trickling down her back.

"So, ye do not wish me to ask if the man ye were chasing escaped?" Iomhar asked, stopping at the edge of the fountain with his foot up on the stone boundary.

"He escaped over the wall," Kit said, gesturing with derision. "He was too quick."

"Aye, I see. Do ye need help getting out of that water, or are your swimming skills strong enough these days?"

"Iomhar!" she snapped, yet it only made him laugh more. "This is not amusing."

"Isn't it? Ye should see my view."

"I am sitting in a fountain whilst God only knows who has escaped. You could run after him."

"Do ye think I would catch him by now?"

"No." She huffed, reluctant to admit it. By now the intruder would have made himself scarce and Iomhar would not know who to look for, regardless.

"Nay. So I'm better off here, offering to help ye out of the fountain."

She threw the cloak in his direction. It was sodden and missed Iomhar's grasp by a few inches, falling into the water in front of him. It splashed him a little, but it did more to spray water over Kit, making her growl in frustration.

"What is this?"

"It's his," Kit said, pushing herself to her feet. "The palace is closed to guests, yet I found him in the garden. When I asked him to show his face, he took off. Clearly, he was unwilling to be seen." When she reached the edge of the fountain, Iomhar offered a hand to help her out, but she thrust it away, jumping down herself. "I do not need your help with everything."

"I know ye do not. It does not mean I cannot offer to help, especially when you have a habit of falling in water."

"I certainly seem to end up in it more than you do."

"But I am not so afraid of it."

"Shh," Kit pleaded, looking around. "I do not need people knowing that."

"Aye, and who is likely to hear us out here? Maybe the lions in the fountain will come alive and tell passing walkers."

"I am not laughing, Iomhar." She reached for the cloak in his grasp and shook it out, conveniently spraying water over him.

He blinked before folding his arms. "Did that help ye to feel better?"

"Immensely." She shook the cloak one last time before something caught her attention on the inside. "Hold this." She thrust it into Iomhar's hands, peeling out the edges.

"I do not think he is still hiding in there."

Kit flapped the material at Iomhar, dampening him further. Then they both smiled a little, looking down at the cloak again. The lining was finely embroidered, far too fine for a simple beggar or worker.

"He must be a man of wealth," she murmured, tracing the golden thread. It formed vines and plants with spiky leaves, before purple thread accented the pointed petals of a flower head. Kit was reminded of the mysterious plant she had seen fastened in one of the herb bundles attached to the ceiling of Queen Elizabeth's chambers. "What is this?" she asked, lifting the embroidered flower up for Iomhar to see.

"A thistle."

"The Scottish flower?" she asked, tilting her head.

"Aye. Did ye not see one when ye were in Edinburgh?" he asked.

Kit shook her head. The only place she could remember seeing it before was in the queen's bedchamber, yet something niggled at her. Was it possible she had seen it somewhere else? "Does it have healing properties?"

"I am the wrong man to ask."

"It's hung in the queen's bedchamber."

"It's Scottish, Kit. Aye, I'd wager money any man who would have *this* sewn inside his cloak was proud of his heritage."

Another part of the embroidery caught Kit's eye. She gathered the cloak up, stuffing more of it into Iomhar's palms.

"What is it?" he asked. "Ye are packing me up like I'm your donkey."

"You can do the same to me another time," Kit said, then straightened out the material, revealing what appeared to be a crest. The golden thread was shaped into a perfect circle, inside which was a bird with a thin beak. It was tilted downward, almost as if the long-necked bird was in prayer, with its wings lifted behind it. It was a bold emblem, as if the bird would take flight at any second. "What is that? A swan?"

"Nay. I know that crest." Iomhar's hands grappled with the cloth. "That is nay swan. It's a pelican."

"A pelican?" Kit wrinkled her nose. She had heard of such birds, but she had never seen one. "What does it mean?" she asked, lifting her eyes to Iomhar.

The mischief in his expression had long gone, replaced with something much darker. Beneath his cropped beard, his lips were flattened together, unmoving, as he stood perfectly still in thought.

"Iomhar?" Kit murmured, trying to rouse him, but he wouldn't respond. He passed his fingers over the crest before gripping it tightly, as if he could crush it. "It would be easier to have an answer from those stone lions at this moment." Kit jerked her head in the direction of the fountain, forcing his eyes back to hers.

"It's the crest of Clan Stuart."

"I beg your pardon?" Her body grew almost as still as his. "The Clan?"

"Aye, they still exist — in remnants, some say, others believe in great bands. It is the clan from which the Scottish kings were born."

"You mean ... Mary Stuart?"

"Aye, just so." Iomhar lifted the crest a little higher. "Whoever wore this is nay friend of our queen's, Kit. They are a friend to Mary Stuart."

Kit turned her eyes to the wall over which the intruder had made his escape. She brushed off the water droplets that were still running down her neck, before turning back to Iomhar.

"We have a Scottish intruder loyal to Mary Stuart. The poisoning. Could they be behind it?"

"But why would they come back to the palace today when she is already poisoned?"

Kit nodded in agreement; it didn't make much sense. "Then I have another question." She breathed deeply, aware that Iomhar was struggling to lift his eyes from the crest. "In Northumberland, what was it Gregorio Luca told us about a supporter of Mary Stuart in London? Someone who was possibly within Hampton Court's walls?" Kit recalled the mission they'd spent in Northumberland, hunting the Jesuit assassin, Luca. Sent to England to attack Queen Elizabeth, Kit and Iomhar were able to track him to the coast of Northumberland, on Holy Island. In exchange for his release to the continent, he told them what he knew of a spy within Hampton Court itself.

Iomhar's fingers tightened around the cloth again as he lowered it between them. "A man in the privy council, and another he had nay knowledge of, except their coded names."

"The Rose and the Lily." Kit shot a glance toward the wall. "What if *he* was one of them?"

A short while later, Kit was standing at the door to the queen's chambers.

"You are drenched," said Lady Hunsdon.

"I will dry," Kit said.

Lady Hunsdon did not move away. She stood firmly in the doorway with her hands on her corseted waist as she stared at Kit. "You are making a puddle on the floor."

"Aye, she is not wrong," Iomhar said from behind Kit. She shot him a glare, trying to urge him to be quiet as she listened to the drips of water that were running off her doublet. It sounded almost as if there was a leak in the timber roof.

"I will dry. My place is in these chambers." Kit tried to move forward again, but Lady Hunsdon stepped in the way. As she stood taller, her ruff twitched, and the red dress quivered with the breath she took.

"Find some new clothes. A gown would be preferable." Lady Hunsdon's dark eyes flicked down to Kit's clothes.

"Daggers are not carried well in a gown," Kit said, hooking her thumbs around the weapons belt. Lady Hunsdon was unmoved, so Kit glanced back at Iomhar, pleading for help.

"Would ye defy the orders of the spymaster, my lady? Kit is to guard the queen."

"Where has she been this last hour, then?"

"Chasing an intruder." Iomhar's words had an effect, for Lady Hunsdon's jaw dropped.

"Did you catch this intruder?" Her question went unanswered, but she seemed to guess the outcome. "Some guard for our queen! She cannot even catch a trespasser."

"We can stand here arguing, my lady, or you can let me return to the queen's side."

"The queen is sick. Do you think bringing in wet clothes will aid her recovery? No." Lady Hunsdon stepped back. "Go home and change. Once you are dry, you can return to your post."

The door closed, so near to Kit's nose that she had to step back in her puddle, nearly colliding with Iomhar. He placed a hand on her back, stopping her from stumbling any further. She jumped away.

"Did I hurt ye?" he asked.

She shook her head. "No, I just was not expecting it." Her words made his brows quirk together. She hurried on, keen not to dwell on the subject. "As she wishes, I must return home to change."

"I thought ye brought clothes with ye?" Iomhar said, stuffing the Scottish cloak he was still carrying under his arm.

"Some, but not enough. I forgot to bring some things." She didn't want to explain to Iomhar why she had left her rooms in such haste. He seemed to sense something was amiss, for his eyes lifted to hers. She looked away. "I will be fast."

"Ye forgot?" he asked, following closely as she rushed down the corridor. "Ye just … forgot?"

"Yes, is that so mad? Maybe I was being absentminded." She tossed the words over her shoulder as she reached a set of steps.

"Absentminded? Nay, that is not a word I'd describe ye with." He was barely a step behind her. "Impulsive, acts without thinking, foolish, aye, these are all words I could use to describe ye —"

"I do not remember inviting an examination of my character. Especially one so unpleasant to listen to."

"I didn't say I thought ill of such things," Iomhar said hurriedly, reaching her side as she jumped the last step to the bottom floor of the palace. "Absentminded, though? Nay. I do not believe that. Why would ye forget to pack something on a commission such as this?"

"Iomhar!" She turned to face him, forcing him to come to a sharp stop. "I merely forgot. It is no incredible thing. I am human and have my foibles as much as the next woman. Now, if you would excuse me." She ran to a side door that led out to the stables beyond the curtain wall, aware that Iomhar was staring after her.

As the cart she requested rode away, leaving the palace behind, Kit looked back. Iomhar quickly left the doorway, retreating into the palace. As the cart moved out into the street and the palace gates closed, a second cart took off from the road, following closely behind. Kit couldn't see who was in the cart, for a hood was pulled tightly over their face, but she suddenly wondered whether the driver of the cart had been waiting for her to leave the palace, or if it was a mere coincidence.

# CHAPTER 8

"Slow down." Kit turned in the cart seat, pulling on the driver's woollen tunic.

"Why?" he asked, flicking his head to the side in alarm.

"There is something I wish to examine." She was careful to keep up an appearance of looking anywhere but behind her, constantly turning her head to the side and looking further back with her eyes alone. The other cart was still following, despite the fact that she had travelled through a myriad of roads and small streets.

It began to slow, with the one mare pulling it forward dropping her nose a little in the reins. Her hooves moved through the trenches of mud beneath her with barely any vigour.

"What are we doing?" the cart driver asked impatiently.

"He should be moving around us."

"What's that?"

It was now clear to her that the cart was following, and she grew more certain when another horse and cart overtook them both.

"At the end of this road, stop," Kit said. The cart pulled up beside where the track banked along the Thames and the road intersected with another, peeling off into the middle of the city. "I will find my way back to the palace."

The cart driver nodded, tugging on the reins to urge the mare to stay still as Kit jumped down from the cart. She hovered for a second, making an appearance of adjusting her clothing as if she hadn't noticed the cart behind them. Out of the corner of her eye, she saw that it had also pulled up and the driver was clambering down. His face was covered by the hood of his cloak, which was tatty and dirty, as if taken from some vagrant or a peg in a stable.

Kit set off down the street. She was careful to walk until her body was completely hidden by the bend in the road. Once she was certain the hooded man from the cart could not see her, she began to run, surprising those wandering the street so much that some yelped and others jumped back, hollering that a boy was disturbing the peace. She tugged her hat lower over her face, glad not to be seen for who she really was. When she reached a crossroads, she glanced back, just enough to see that the hooded man was catching up. His hood had fallen down, but beneath he wore a hat, making his face undiscernible at this distance.

Kit was too busy looking behind her to keep track of where her feet were going. As she sprinted, she found herself in a road.

"Watch out!"

"Stop the boy!"

Cries went up, calling for her. She whipped round, trying not to think about whether it was soil or horse manure beneath her feet, when she saw a cart coming toward her, the steed pulling so hard and fast that the driver couldn't stop in time. He wailed for her to get out of the way and hauled on the reins.

Kit turned, trying to flee to the other side of the road. She narrowly escaped the horse, but the cart was wider, and she was clipped by the wood. It knocked her from her feet, sending her to the ground. Rolling through the mud, the dirt splattered across her cheeks and caked the end of her nose.

"Someone help him up!"

"Is the lad hurt?"

"Is he alive?"

Kit ignored all the cries of panic, thinking only of the pain that ricocheted through the arm that she had landed on. It was sharp and pronounced, with something twanging deep within her elbow.

"You all right, boy?" a voice asked, much closer to her ear than she had expected. A pair of hands pulled her to her feet. She winced at the tug on her arm.

"I am well, thank you," she said hurriedly, glancing back across the road. She was now separated from her pursuer by a line of carriages, yet his head was visible from where he had stopped on the other side of the road. Part of his hat was discernible too. It was possibly the same hat the intruder in Hampton Court gardens had worn, though she could not be certain.

"Take a minute, boy. You might be hurt." The man beside her was trying to encourage her to be still, but she was already backing out of his hold.

"I am well. Thank you again," she said before she took off, clinging to her injured arm. The more she ran, the more painful it grew, and she had to work hard to keep it still, though she didn't stop. She kept looking back, beginning to think she had escaped her pursuer, but she didn't let herself believe it, not yet.

The memory of Newcastle was too much. All of it was fresh and driving her forward. She could still picture the moment her attacker had tried to hurt her with a billhook, and she had driven a blade into his side. She didn't want to relive it.

Running as fast as she could through the streets, she worked a strange path to her lodgings, being careful not to go there directly. She feared that death would be waiting for her round every corner, with a billhook in his hands.

As the cart pulled up outside Hampton Court, Kit looked down at her arm. The skin had been torn open and blood was seeping out, though she'd tried to bind the wound with her shirt sleeve.

"Nasty thing you got there, flap."

Kit bristled at the word and turned toward the cart driver sitting beside her.

"You need to get it seen to." He looked away. "On your way. Got places I need to go."

Kit jumped down from the cart, pulling the jerkin up over her shoulders to hide the wound. "Flap," she murmured, repeating the word. She had heard it often enough, sometimes as a way to refer to those ladies that perhaps sold themselves in the night. She cursed under her breath and turned away, heading through the main gate of Hampton Court. It seemed that strangers were fond of finding other names for her besides her own. She glanced down at the clothes she wore, knowing it had to be because of the way she dressed.

"Kit? Is that ye?" Iomhar's voice broke through the chatter in the base courtyard.

Kit looked round, seeing a group of men in the centre of the cobbles. Most she recognised as working for Walsingham, whilst others were dressed in the yeoman's and gentlemen-at-arm's robes, all bright red and black. Amongst them, Iomhar was breaking free of the conversation, coming to talk to her.

"Ye weren't long."

"No." Kit spoke hurriedly, being careful to hold her injured arm behind her back. If the blood seeped through the jerkin as well as the shirt, she didn't want to give Iomhar the chance to see it. "I am needed here, am I not?"

"Aye." Iomhar stopped a short distance from her and cocked his head to the side. "What is it? What is wrong?"

She did her best to scoff and turn away. "Nothing is wrong. Why would you think something is wrong?" she said over her shoulder, aware that Iomhar was following her across the cobbled courtyard, toward the second gatehouse in the palace.

"Ye think I do not know ye well enough by now to know when ye are lying?" Iomhar laughed as he caught up with her. He cut in front, blocking her path.

"You do not know me as well as you think you do, Iomhar." She walked around him, continuing toward the second gate tower.

Iomhar kept pace with her. "Independently minded, impetuous and impulsive too. Ye would much rather bicker with me than have a normal conversation; though ye pretend ye do not like it, ye clearly do. Ye are stormy and quiet when something is bothering ye. Ye would rather drink mead than ale, ye'd rather use manchet bread for a seat than to eat it, and your favourite food is marchpane."

The words pulled Kit to a sharp stop before the gatehouse door. She turned on the spot to face him, with her lips slightly parted. Iomhar stood taller, his chin high.

"How did I do?" he asked.

"Not bad," she said, trying to keep the smile from her face. "You are wrong on one count, though."

"What is that?"

"Ravel is my least favourite bread, not manchet." She turned away as Iomhar cursed under his breath. She came face to face with a yeoman, who was evidently reluctant to let her pass. "Kit Scarlett, you saw me pass you by earlier."

The man remembered her as soon as she spoke.

"Yes, the sheep in wolf's clothing." He stepped to the side. Kit shot a dark glare at him before she walked on, with Iomhar rushing behind.

"Ye going to tell me what is wrong yet?" he asked, following her up a set of stone steps that passed through a doorway, leading to another set of stairs, this one made out of dark oak wood.

"Let us say I am tired of the comments being made today."

"Such as the wolf's clothing?"

"Yes. I have also been called a flap and an unnatural woman." She tried to laugh, shaking her head. "Take me back to the countryside, Iomhar. They did not care if they passed someone who was a little different."

"Gladly. Kit, wait." He reached out and took her arm.

Kit winced, for he had taken hold of the wound unknowingly. He instantly released it, looking down at her in surprise.

"What is that?" he asked, reaching for the sleeve of her jerkin.

She freed her arm before he could pull back the sleeve. "It is just a bruise. I walked into the timbers in my rooms." Further on down the corridor, there was a sound. Kit turned her head toward it, seeing more yeomen were walking, three astride down the corridor. Behind them were two of the ladies-in-waiting, talking in surprisingly cheery tones.

Kit lifted a hand, silently pleading with Iomhar to stay quiet as the ladies and the yeomen passed her. When they drew level, Kit could see their faces. One was Lady Bess of Hardwick, her large form practically shuddering with laughter as she passed. The other was Lady Eleanor Gifford, trying to hide her giggle behind a lifted hand. Once they were gone, passing down the staircase behind Kit, she turned to Iomhar to see his face was as wan and confused as her own.

"I do not understand. How can they laugh when their queen is on her deathbed?"

"You stole my very thought." Kit nodded at him. "I need to get back to the queen. Have you found the gunpowder yet?"

"Nay." Iomhar shook his head. "Walsingham seems to think it was a lie."

"Maybe it was. Or maybe not." Kit walked away, heading along the corridor and looping her injured arm in front of her. Iomhar said nothing, but she was aware he didn't walk off, not straight away. He stayed exactly where he was, staring after her.

Kit passed through into the great hall, stepping under wooden archways that were still carved with the previous king's initial, H. She strode across the hall with the ornately carved ceiling high above her head. Through a far doorway, the rooms peeled off into small corridors. Kit took the slimmest one, heading for the queen's rooms.

When she reached the chamber with the gentleman-at-arms standing guard, she nodded in greeting and stepped inside.

The privy chamber was not as she had left it. Gone was the peace and quiet murmuring that had previously filled this space. Instead, there was uproar, with voices practically shrill.

"Have you not seen her?" a first voice cried.

As Kit closed the door behind her, she turned to see Miss Radcliff, her face flushed and her hands waving in fear.

"One would have to be blind not to see the state she is in."

"Be quiet, girl." Lady Hunsdon stepped forward. "We are not blind, and the queen is not deaf. She may be behind two doors, but with such shrill squeals, I'd wager money she can hear you."

Kit stepped forward, looking between the ladies-in-waiting. The sound of her boots on the floor prompted Lady Hunsdon to look her way.

"You have returned, I see." She was clearly attempting to adopt a calm manner as she spoke, but Kit's eyes flitted down to the hands that were fidgeting madly, twisting at her wide skirt.

"What has happened?"

"What happens here is the queen's business," Lady Hunsdon said dismissively and turned away. She retreated to her closest friend in the room, Lady Stafford, who began to whisper in her ear.

"The queen's business is the state's business. I do not need to give you a lecture on that, Lady Hunsdon." Kit had had enough. She strode forward, keeping her wounded arm behind her back in case the bleeding grew worse. "What has happened?"

Lady Hunsdon opened her lips, clearly angry, but her friend elbowed her.

"Tell her." For the first time, Lady Stafford's voice was loud enough for Kit to hear her.

"I will show her instead." Lady Hunsdon stepped away from her friend and beckoned Kit to follow her to the withdrawing chamber. Once inside, she lifted the net curtain that separated them from the queen.

She was sleeping on her bed, with nothing but one candle beside her to light her still face. The wheezing was evident, more laboured than before, and the face had become almost skeletal.

"She's dying," Kit whispered, so only Lady Hunsdon could hear her.

"She is losing the battle with the poison," Lady Hunsdon muttered, her fingers fussing with the net curtain as she shook.

"Or…" Kit trailed off as a thought struck her. The downturn was so sudden from when she had seen her earlier that day, she knew there was another explanation. It was possible that the queen had been poisoned again.

# CHAPTER 9

"Are you going to tell me what happened?" Morgan asked as he bound Kit's wound. She looked around the withdrawing chamber, relieved that the ladies were all so busy in their panic and conversation in the privy chamber, that they had not noticed she had borrowed the apothecary.

"It was a cart accident, that is all," Kit murmured before grimacing at the pain.

"A little longer, and we will be done." The apothecary bound what appeared to be long leaves over her wound, followed by thin linen bandages.

"What is all this?" Kit whispered, sniffing the wound. It had a particularly strong scent.

"Maudlinwort, cleavers and plantain."

"They smell pungent." She looked away, blinking at the sting in her eyes. She cursed, knowing it would be difficult to keep the wound a secret from Iomhar and Walsingham if she had to go around everywhere smelling so strongly.

"This cart accident, was that all it was?" Morgan asked as he finished and sat back.

"Yes." Kit stood, showing the conversation was at an end. "Thank you for your help, sir." She walked away and moved to the net curtain that separated her from the queen. The constant questions were bothering her.

The last time she had been chased, her pursuer had been intent on killing her. Iomhar had insisted on sending her somewhere safe, and she couldn't bear for that to be repeated. She was at Hampton Court for a purpose, after all. She had to protect the queen, and she wasn't going to risk being turned away from this position.

"What do you think, Miss Scarlett?" the apothecary asked as he came to stand with Kit, in the doorway of the queen's privy chamber. "Do you think she is losing the fight? Her state has certainly worsened."

"What has she eaten since this morning?" Kit asked. Lady Stafford was sitting silently at the queen's side, her hand in hers as quiet tears rolled down her cheeks.

"Nothing. She has only drunk a tonic I myself have provided."

"I see." Kit kept her thoughts to herself as she glanced at the apothecary, realising she didn't know who she could trust in that room. "Where is the tonic now?"

"By her bed." Morgan pointed to a small oak table, separated from the queen by one of the red curtains that draped the bed. On top was a tiny glass vial, no bigger than a thumb and with less than half the liquid left inside it.

Kit stepped further into the room, prompting Lady Stafford to look at her with alarm. Kit parted her lips, ready to come up with an excuse for her entrance, when a *boom* echoed across the chamber.

Kit's legs froze, her hand reaching out for the doorframe beside her. The wood shook as a feeling of thunder echoed around the building. Lady Stafford gripped the bed. Behind Kit, the apothecary yelped, clinging to the other side of the doorframe.

"What is that?" he asked, his voice quaking. "Is the earth shaking?"

Kit stepped away from the door. She went to the other end of the room, where a lead-latticed window overlooked one of the courtyards of the palace. In the courtyard there was uproar, with some of the yeomen looking at each other and wildly asking what had happened. One of the yeomen thrust a finger at the sky.

"Up there!" he called.

Kit followed the motioning arm to see that billows of smoke were filling the air. It formed rather like a beast with its shoulders rolling backwards.

"W-What is it?" Lady Stafford stammered.

"An explosion." Kit stepped away from the window as she spoke, not wanting to believe it. "The gunpowder."

"Gunpowder? What gunpowder?" the apothecary asked, stepping forward.

"Stay with her. Do not leave the queen unguarded," Kit ordered the two of them and ran out of the room.

The ladies in the privy chamber were now in chaos for different reasons, clinging to one another and staring at the walls as if they were about to come down on them.

"Let no one in through that door except me, understood?" Kit said to the room. When no lady answered her, she turned in the final doorway, seeking out Lady Hunsdon. "Lady Hunsdon, is that understood?"

The ageing face lifted, revealing fear. She nodded slowly.

"Good." Kit left the room, closing the door harshly behind her. She reached out for the gentleman-at-arms who stood by the door with his sword limp in his hands. She took hold of his sleeve and shook him into focus. "That will do no good against an explosion."

"Explosion?" he repeated, his eyes darting up, clearly in shock.

"Stay here. Do not move from this door."

"Yes, sir, I mean, ma'am."

Kit shot him a warning look before she fled down the corridor. She hurried through the rooms, looking out for any strangers that might have been lurking in the corridors, yet there was no one. The staircase was empty, and the great hall merely had yeomen inside, all peering out of the windows and pointing in wonder at the smoke billowing in the air.

When Kit reached the first courtyard, she darted toward the narrow passage to the kitchens, marking the others ahead of her, each one rushing toward the site of the explosion. Kit fled through an archway into a tiny lane squashed between two walls of the palace. They raced through Fish Court and past the boiler house, where hurried feet began to slow at the sight unveiling in front of them. The roof of the kitchens had a hole in the top, tiles were missing, and three tall red chimneys were at an angle, with one at risk of falling over.

When she reached the door of the kitchens it was open, with scullery and kitchen maids running out, some with blackened hands and one with a blackened face. The latter walked straight, with no tears and no words passing her lips. Kit reached for the girl and shook her.

"Are you hurt?" Kit cried. At first, the girl didn't answer; she just continued to stare forward. "Speak to me!" Kit begged, shaking her again. The girl's eyes flicked to Kit, as her soul seemed to return to her body.

"No," she murmured. "But they are." She pointed back into the kitchen.

"Can you tell me what happened?" Kit asked.

"He picked up the rat."

"The rat?"

"The boy who watches the fire. He found a rat." She pointed down at the cobbles, as if the rat had run between them now.

"He picked it up and threw it on the fire, but then it…" She gestured with her hands, splaying her fingers outward.

"I understand. Find yourself some water." Kit urged the girl forward again. The other maids came to collect their friend, taking her arms and dragging her away through the lane.

Kit stepped through the doorway, finding the air was filling with smoke fast. She lifted her arm and covered her mouth with her sleeve, blocking out the acrid fumes. She hastened through the corridor, passing storage rooms and a chamber filled with barrels of ale.

"Get them out of here! Aye, ye, take him that way. Get him to the physician in the stable quarters. Now." Iomhar's voice made Kit hesitate as she rounded a corner into the kitchens.

Before her, a black world appeared. What had once been a busy kitchen with high white walls was now covered in soot. The dark roof had a hole in the top, filled with escaping smoke. There was the carcass of a fireplace in which the fire was still raging, barely contained by the remains of the stone surround. The flames were licking up the ceiling, climbing higher and higher.

"Bring down the tiles." Iomhar was in the middle of the kitchen, issuing orders. "Bring water from the Thames." Men followed his commands, darting out of another door at the far side of the room.

"Iomhar?" Kit called.

He turned, his eyes searching for her as the sounds of wood cracking overhead echoed around the room. "Get back, Kit!" he yelled, running toward her. She jumped back into the doorway as Iomhar reached her.

The ceiling came down, the wood shattering into fragments. It was such a crash that she could hear nothing else, only a ringing sound that seemed to be inside her head. As splinters of wood and smoke filled the air, Kit felt arms around her. It took only a second for her to realise that Iomhar was pushing her further into the corridor that led to the kitchen, urging her against the far wall and shielding her with his body. She couldn't fight against him, nor rail that she didn't need his protection, for the falling wood was too loud, and it just kept going. She was also glad of it at this moment. She gripped Iomhar's arms, trying to look up into his face, but she could see nothing but black.

Then the sounds stopped abruptly, before intense coughing began. Not just from the few people who were still in the kitchen, but from Iomhar and Kit too. Kit felt the smoke curling around her throat and choking her. Kit blinked once as light filtered through the blackness, her vision beginning to clear.

"Window, Kit," Iomhar managed to say. He leaned against the wall beside her head, giving Kit just enough room to look behind her. There was indeed a window there. The closest to it, she pushed against the glass, but the frame was too hot to move, and the glass was no longer in one piece, having shattered in the explosion. Kit braced herself and lifted her elbow, smashing through what was left. At once, fresh air filled the room. Kit and Iomhar thrust their heads through the gap.

"How many are in there?" she called to him.

"Three that I last saw. We need to get them out. Before the wee man above brings down more of the ceiling."

Kit took a deep breath and held it, lifting her sleeve over her face as she turned in the corridor and headed back through the archway into the kitchen. Iomhar was behind her, doing the same thing.

As the smoke and ash began to dissipate from the air, Kit caught sight of blackened pots and smashed pickling vessels that had been thrown into the far wall by the explosion. A patch of the floor was covered in debris from the ceiling, with great timbers snapped into fragments. Beneath these timbers there were three people, only two of which Kit could see.

She ran forward, reaching for the one closest to her and lifting the pieces of timber off the man's stomach. He wailed at the pain, clutching his chest. Kit was pleased to see the yeoman wasn't bleeding, though perhaps he had broken ribs and bruises.

"Take my hand," she said to him, coughing. He reached out as she pulled him to his feet. "Can you walk?"

"Just." He pushed past her, heading for the door.

Kit looked around to see Iomhar had freed another person, but this man's leg was bent in the wrong direction. Iomhar lifted him over his shoulder.

"I have ye. Don't worry," Iomhar said, his voice loud enough to be heard over the roar of the flames.

Kit looked around, searching for the last person in the room. A whimper to her left brought a pile of timber to her attention, packed so high that it masked whoever was beneath it. She started lifting off the pieces, and eventually a small hand appeared.

"I'm going to pull you out," she called, beginning to tug. To her surprise, it was no man, but a skinny boy. Blood was seeping down one side of his head and there was soot across the other side. His clothes had been badly burned, so much so that there was barely anything left of the white apron around his waist apart from the tie. "Can you walk?"

He nodded, though he said nothing, doing his best to stumble free of the timber. When he nearly fell over, Kit threw him over her shoulder and hurried out of the room, taking the corridor toward the small space that marked the entry to the cobbled lane at Fish Court.

There were many people gathered in that small space, with lots of worried faces and trembling hands reaching toward the injured. As Kit placed the boy down on the ground, Iomhar appeared at her side, just in time to catch the boy as he fell backward.

"Woah, ye are all right, lad. We have ye," Iomhar said, his voice soothing. Kit kneeled before the boy as Iomhar lowered him softly to the ground. He too was covered in soot, but his green eyes were alert, never wavering from the boy. "Are ye injured?"

"No." The boy spoke slowly as he looked up from his burnt clothes. "It was the rat."

Kit bent toward him, remembering what the young scullery maid had said. "You were the boy that threw the rat on the fire?" she asked slowly.

"Yes. I ... I thought it was dead." His voice was growing panicked. "Then it just... I don't know what it did. The rat was there and then it exploded —"

"Calm yourself, lad." Iomhar placed a hand on the boy's shoulder. It seemed to have a calming effect, for the boy's body stopped shuddering, and he took a deep breath. "There ye go, just keep breathing. Now, this rat. Ye said it was dead?"

"It did not move."

Iomhar sat back, his eyes lifting to Kit's. She knew that look; she had seen it often enough before.

"You know what this is, do you not?" she asked warily.

"Aye," he nodded. "I have seen it once before."

# CHAPTER 10

"Say that again, Iomhar — only whisper it, for the blood of the Lord's sake," Walsingham muttered angrily, beckoning Iomhar and Kit to the side of the courtyard.

Kit looked back and forth, from the mad dash of people heading to the kitchens, all still trying to attend to the wounded and clear up the blast, then back to Iomhar. His cheeks were blackened, and his hair practically stood on end at the back. She suspected she looked much the same.

"Are ye scared someone will hear?" Iomhar asked, his eyes narrowing. "Let them hear, it doesn't change what happened."

"Kit, make him listen," said Walsingham. "I do not want others to hear of this. We do not need this palace in uproar."

"I think that would be shutting the door after the horse has very much bolted," Kit murmured and gestured over her shoulder at the men running across the courtyard. Some had buckets of water and others had metal hooks attached to ropes, designed to pull down the bricks and stop the fire from spreading. "He will not listen to me anyway."

"I don't always bend to her will, Walsingham." Iomhar's voice had turned dark.

"Do you not?" Walsingham shook his head, clearly disbelieving him.

"This conversation is not helping us." Kit spoke quickly, holding her hands up between the two men. Walsingham's gaunt face grew even more pinched, whilst Iomhar's lips flickered into the smallest of smiles, as if he had won the argument. "Iomhar, are you certain of this? Of the rat?"

"I saw it once on the continent." He held out his hands and curled one into a fist, as if it were the rat they were discussing. "All ye need is a dead rat, and an incision across his back, here." He drew a line across his knuckles. "Put a small bag of gunpowder inside and stitch the fur together once more. Then ye leave the rat near a fire, for what does everyone do when they see a dead rat near an open grate?"

"They throw it on the flames." Kit gritted her teeth. "It was an attack on the kitchens."

"Aye, I believe it was."

"Why, though? The threat of the gunpowder was against the queen, not her kitchens."

"It was also too small a blast to kill. Injure, aye, maim too. There are many that will be limping away from that kitchen, but kill? Nay. That was not the purpose of that blast. There was nay way of them knowing that it would bring part of the roof down." Iomhar shook his head, looking out to the courtyard.

"Then what was the purpose?" Walsingham asked impatiently. "Why would anyone want to blow up the kitchens?"

Iomhar stepped back, his focus on the kitchens and the smoke pluming into the sky.

"Now he's walking away." Walsingham flapped, turning to Kit for help. "Kit, what is the matter with him? Has he lost the power of his tongue?"

"Walsingham, calm." Kit took his arm, but it did little good. His cheeks were turning puce, and his hands were so restless that she could see the sinews moving beneath the skin. "I will talk to him." Kit turned away, only to find Iomhar had increased the distance between them. He had walked into the centre of the courtyard and was staring up at the smoke that was beginning to dissipate a little. No longer a thin black plume, it was spreading its wings, turning the bright wintery sky an unnatural shade of grey. "Iomhar?" Kit whispered as she reached his side.

"Kit, think on it. Where is everyone looking at the moment in this palace?" he said, never taking his eyes off the smoke. "It's the perfect distraction, is it not? An explosion like this. I warrant there are parts of the palace that are empty."

"You mean … the attack was not designed to hurt anyone but could have been designed to distract us all?" Kit turned around, her eyes flitting between the windows of Hampton Court. "What are they doing, then? If they were already in the kitchens, then they have access here. They were not breaking in."

"What if they were bringing something in?" Iomhar looked over his shoulder at Kit. "We didn't find anything in the search, aye?"

"That is what you said."

"What if we were looking too soon?" he asked. "What if the gunpowder is only just being brought in now?"

Kit took a step back, searching the windows once more. By the time they gathered the yeomen and the intelligencers to block off all the doors and windows, whoever could be bringing in such quantities of gunpowder could have achieved their aim.

"Then the palace could be blown up any minute." She chewed her lip. "Walsingham?" she called as the spymaster hobbled forward from where he had been leaning on the red-brick wall of the palace. "We have to move the queen."

"Move her?" Walsingham said. His black heeled shoes slipped sideways, before righting themselves again. He held his hands open and looked between Kit and Iomhar, as if they had grown hooves. "Have you become a fool before my eyes, Kit? You think that our queen is capable of moving?"

"No," Kit said with a sigh, "but I fear we have no choice."

"She cannot be moved." The physician was emphatic as he looked between Kit and Walsingham.

"We must consider it," Walsingham said slowly. He wiped the back of his sleeve across his head, mopping away the sweat trickling down his temple, despite the chill in the queen's privy chamber.

"Move her? No." Lady Hunsdon approached, leaving the other ladies who were gathered in one corner. "Moving Her Majesty could kill her."

"Staying here could kill her too, and in a way that is much more horrific," Kit said stoically, earning a sharp elbow in her ribs from Walsingham.

"That does not help us, Kit," he murmured.

"What does Lord Burghley say?" the physician asked, looking between the two of them. Kit glanced at Walsingham, seeing the way a muscle around his eye twitched, showing that he was concealing something. Kit knew Lord Burghley hadn't yet been told. There had not been time to find him.

"He *will* agree with me. There is a threat in these palace walls," Walsingham declared with vigour and gestured to the window. "Do you want to see another such explosion in this place? Do you want Her Majesty to be here when it happens?"

"It was merely an accident, surely," Lady Hunsdon said quietly. "We heard a kitchen boy made a mistake."

"What kind of kitchen mistake could cause such an explosion? There was no mistake." Kit stood a little taller as she spoke, feeling Lady Hunsdon's harsh gaze swivel toward her. "It was intended."

"By whom?"

"We do not know." Yet Kit's mind was on the intruder dressed in the Scottish cloak.

"Walsingham?" Lady Hunsdon turned her eyes on him. "Is this not your realm? Are you not the one supposed to keep the demons from the queen's front door?"

"They are not just at the front door," Kit answered before Walsingham could. "They are inside the palace, crawling through the walls and probably hiding in the shadows of this very chamber —"

"How dare you insinuate that not everyone in this room can be trusted!" Lady Hunsdon's words echoed off the walls, and she was hushed by the other ladies. She glanced toward them, breathing deeply as a bull preparing to charge, before looking back to Kit.

"Sometimes the threat is nearer than any of us fear it to be, my lady," Walsingham said and took hold of Kit's arm, gripping it tightly to stop her from saying any more. "This is not up for discussion. The queen must be told and as soon as she is well enough to be moved, we will move her." Walsingham looked between Lady Hunsdon and the physician, evidently waiting for an answer. The physician soon nodded and retreated to a corner of the room, but Lady Hunsdon said nothing at all. "Come, we will tell her now."

Walsingham let go of Kit and stepped toward the door, instructing Kit to follow with a wave of his hand, but Lady Hunsdon stepped in her way.

"Kit?" Walsingham called impatiently.

"I am needed, my lady," Kit said, attempting to walk around her. But it wasn't long before more ladies gathered in her path. Either side of Lady Hunsdon, Lady Stafford, Miss Parry and Miss Radcliff stood up. On the other side of the room, Lady

Hardwick and Lady Gifford were giggling, watching her closely.

"We do not approve of you being so close to the queen," Lady Hunsdon said. "We think it wise you do not go into the privy chamber in future."

"That is not your decision to make. That is Walsingham's decision, or the queen's." Kit spoke slowly, not looking away from Lady Hunsdon. Instead of walking around the ladies, she walked straight between them, pushing Lady Hunsdon's and Miss Parry's shoulders to get by. Miss Parry complained at the pain of it, whilst Lady Hunsdon urged her to be quiet.

As Kit stepped into the withdrawing chamber, she found Walsingham standing in the doorway to the private chamber, lifting the white net to gaze at the queen.

"Is something amiss with the ladies?" Walsingham whispered as Kit moved closer.

"They do not like me. That is all."

"Why not?" Walsingham asked, frowning a little.

"Something about me being an *unnatural* woman, I think. That is what Lady Hunsdon says." Kit shrugged when Walsingham's gaze softened. "She is protective of her queen, that I can understand, even if I cannot understand the insult."

Walsingham nodded and gestured for Kit to lead the way into the chamber. She crossed to the other side of the bed, aware that as she moved, one of the ladies hurried through the withdrawing chamber to follow them. Standing on the other side of the queen's bed, Kit hovered as Lady Stafford took a seat beside the queen, reaching for her hand.

Kit could feel the small table on her other side, on which the small vial of tonic the apothecary had provided was placed. Kit moved to conceal the vial from view.

"Can she speak at present?" Walsingham stood opposite Kit, with his eyes on Lady Stafford. In answer, she merely shook her head.

Walsingham took a stool next to the queen and leaned toward her. She angled her head to him in recognition, but she said nothing. Her normally pink lips were grey, curling back across her teeth. Her eyes, however, were alert, constantly shifting across his face and the bedclothes around her.

"I do not doubt you have been told of the explosion, Your Majesty," Walsingham began slowly, his manner now calm. "You should know that we believe it is no accident. We think someone is bringing gunpowder into the palace, with the intention of murder."

The queen's breath hitched. Lady Stafford gripped her hand tighter.

"We have men completing another search of the palace as we speak, led by one of my own intelligencers, but if we are to do so thoroughly, it will take some time. In the meantime, we must consider moving you."

A sound passed the queen's lips and she shook her head. She then rolled over in the bed, turning away from Walsingham.

"I understand, Your Majesty," he said, his voice gentler than Kit could recall it ever being. "If you are too weak to be moved, then we must stay." Kit flicked her gaze up to him, seeing the softness in his face, and was reminded of something that had passed between them long ago.

She'd been in Seething Lane, sick with great wheezing coughs that had filled the building, right up to the beamed rafters. Walsingham had been gentle with her that day. She'd been no taller than his hip, sitting with him by the fire with her face bent over a steaming bowl of water that Doris had prepared. She'd been wearing a gown, still so young that she hadn't yet tried men's clothes. Walsingham had stayed with her throughout, refusing to leave her side, and even letting her fall asleep with her head resting on his knee.

There was a glimmer of that man now as he reached out and placed a hand on the queen's shoulder. It was too familiar a touch for someone of royal blood, so much so that Kit thought she would push him off her, but she didn't. The queen's breath merely deepened, as if she was comforted by that touch for a few seconds.

As Walsingham stepped back, he nodded once at Kit. They had their answer — the queen could not move. As he turned his back and left the room, Lady Stafford stood. This gave Kit the opportunity that she needed. She looked round to see the glass vial, still half full of tonic. Checking to see Lady Stafford wasn't looking her way, Kit snatched the vial and thrust it deep in her pocket, before following the two of them out of the chamber.

# CHAPTER 11

"What is that, Kit?"

Kit didn't look up from the vial. Awake all night by the queen's side, now that dawn had come she was sitting on a quiet staircase in the palace, having been given a few resting hours. Leaning on the banister, she tipped the liquid in the vial back and forth.

"Ye with me or asleep?" Iomhar asked as he sat down beside her, with such a heavy thud that she lifted her head and turned to look at him.

He was no longer covered in ash and debris from the blast, but there were heavy shadows under his eyes, marking his sleeplessness. He leaned back, resting his head on the nosing of one of the steps above them.

"I am barely awake," Kit murmured, yawning as she mirrored his position. As she lowered the vial to her lap, she looked above them. Beside the staircase was a tall window that stretched the height of the building. Narrow and full of lead latticework, it filled the staircase with early-morning light, casting the steps in an apricot-tinged glow. "Did you find anything in the search?"

"Aye, that's why I'm lying here, celebrating," Iomhar jested, though his voice lacked vigour.

Lacking the energy to laugh, Kit merely smiled and reached out a hand, tapping him on the arm. "Not a thing? No trace of gunpowder?"

"Nay." He rubbed his palms over his face, before scoring his nails across his cheeks, where his two white scars sat. "This is maddening, Kit. I am certain that explosion was a distraction; nothing else makes sense."

"I know." She turned her gaze to the window through which the light streamed in. "I think you could be right, about someone sneaking in the gunpowder, but I do not imagine they would make it easy for us to find. It would not surprise me if we searched for weeks and never found it."

"They have good ideas of where to hide it, I'll give them that." Iomhar sighed and let his arms drop. His hand brushed Kit's, surprising her enough to snatch hers away, resting it on her stomach. "Ye act like my touch hurts ye, Kit."

"That is not what I was doing," she said hurriedly, closing her eyes.

"Aye, course not." He shifted on the stairs and turned his head toward her. "What is that?" He pointed down at the vial.

"It is the apothecary's tonic, but there is something strange to it." She held up the vial so Iomhar could see the liquid in the sunlight. "It is the same as the vial I found on her bureau. Do you see this white powder hovering between the herbs?"

Iomhar took the vial from her and twisted it back and forth, watching as a white sediment shifted through the green leaves that were suspended in the liquid. "Bloody hell, Kit. Are ye telling me ye think the queen is being continuously poisoned?"

"I think it is possible. It would account for her deteriorating state."

"By the apothecary?" Iomhar asked, sitting up straight in his alarm.

"No. That would hardly make sense. He is the one person I am certain did not do it. He told us that he suspected the queen was being poisoned. No poisoner would draw attention to that, would they?"

"Nay, I suppose not." Iomhar lay down again, still playing with the vial. "So? What are your thoughts?"

"We are looking for someone who had access to the queen's withdrawing chamber before she fell ill, and after, in order to administer it both in the daily tonic and this medicine. I think that leads us to only one possible solution. I think…" she whispered, pausing to check she could hear no sounds of anyone walking by in the corridors, "it is one of her ladies-in-waiting."

Iomhar's eyebrows lifted sharply. "Ye are certain?" he asked.

Kid nodded slowly. "They are the only ones who always have access to those rooms. It is one of them, I am sure of it." In her mind, Kit could see all the faces. She could see the fierce protectiveness of Lady Hunsdon and the quiet manners of Lady Stafford. There were the eager attentions of Miss Parry and Miss Radcliff too, then the pair that were always laughing together, Lady Hardwick and Lady Gifford.

"Which one, Kit?" Iomhar asked.

Kit didn't reply at first. She found it hard to believe that Lady Hunsdon and Lady Stafford could fake their devotion to the queen, especially as they had been by her side for decades. Yet loyalties could change.

"Kit?" Iomhar elbowed her and she flinched. "For the wee man's sake, Kit. I am not going to make ye ill by touching ye."

"You made me jump, that is all."

"Ye are a poor liar sometimes," Iomhar muttered before he slid along the staircase, putting distance between them. Kit looked down at the gap, unable to explain why it saddened her. "Which lady, Kit? Which lady do ye suspect?"

"What do you know of Lady Hardwick?" Kit asked, lifting herself up onto her elbows, the better to look at Iomhar.

"Bess of Hardwick? Aye, many whispers about her across London, are there not?" He shook his head, seeming amused. "Who really kens what is truth and what is creation? They say she has a stormy relationship with the queen. They can be the most devoted friends, and then distanced from one another, writing just once a year. They argue too."

"You seem to know a lot."

"Only whispers I have heard. It could all be rumours. I once heard Walsingham talk cautiously of her. He said it was unclear, after years of holding Mary Stuart under house arrest, just where Lady Hardwick's loyalties were."

"What?" Kit sat further forward. "Lady Hardwick is the one who keeps Mary Stuart locked up?"

"Not right now." Iomhar shook his head. "She did for many years, I believe. Did ye not know?"

"No." Kit sat forward and took the vial back from Iomhar, peering at the contents again. "If Walsingham does not trust her, why is she in the queen's chambers?"

"I hear she is here after separating from her husband."

Kit nodded, remembering she had heard such a thing from the gossip whispered between the ladies.

"Perhaps the queen overruled Walsingham's opinion," Iomhar offered, sitting back on the stairs.

"It is possible," Kit nodded slowly. "She could have access to the room, and she is certainly fond of laughing and gossiping, much more so than watching over her supposed friend."

"Ye do not like her much, do ye?"

"I could not shake my head emphatically enough for that one," Kit murmured, earning a deep chuckle from Iomhar. It was the way Lady Hardwick laughed when the queen was so weakened that left Kit cold.

"Walsingham said she has a cleverness to her. One that ye cannot always see, but do not underestimate her."

Kit blinked and pocketed the glass vial. She felt the danger closing in. "We cannot give up searching for that gunpowder yet, Iomhar." She stood up.

Iomhar groaned from behind her. "Can I have five minutes first?"

Kit reached back and took his hand. Clearly the touch surprised him, for he snapped his head up off the steps.

"No, you cannot." She pulled him to his feet.

"I'll wager everything I own there is nay gunpowder in here."

"I am tempted to take that wager," Kit murmured as she opened the door of the ale cellar and stepped inside. Iomhar followed, their only light being the candle that was clutched in his hands. "I rather like the idea of living in that big house of yours, if you are so willing to wager it."

"Ye should try it some time. It's rather empty when there is nay one else in it."

"You have your cook."

"Aye, and Elspeth prefers to stay in the other part of the house. Believe me, Kit. A great house is not everything ye think it is."

"Then we could swap," Kit said with a laugh. "I will have the house and you can have my attic rooms."

"With the faulty lock on the door? Nay, I will pass."

Kit lifted up the lids of the ale barrels, peering inside. Each barrel she checked proved as fruitless as the last. "You were right," she said, sighing as she walked back out of the ale room into a long, narrow corridor in the cellar, beneath the belly of the palace.

"Aye, this place gets too many people to hide something here. If I was going to hide a barrel of gunpowder somewhere, it would be quieter than this." He followed her into the corridor as Kit heard a sound, rather like the door of the cellar at the top of the staircase opening. "Does that mean I win the wager? Good, as much as I do not like the big house, I don't fancy sleeping on the street tonight."

"Shh." Kit waved her hand at Iomhar.

"Ye are just shushing me because ye lost."

"Iomhar." She turned and stood on her toes, placing her hand over his mouth. Iomhar froze, staring at her with his green eyes narrowed. Kit gestured down the corridor with a jerk of her head, and Iomhar's gaze flicked to the side.

Kit knew no one was permitted in the cellars whilst the search was underway, so who was coming down the stairs?

All was black around them, apart from the solitary candle that Iomhar had in his hand. By that light, they could just about see a shadow at the far end of the corridor. It was hurrying down the cellar steps toward the corridor where they stood.

Iomhar pushed the candle toward Kit's lips, and she blew out the flame, casting them into darkness.

Down the cellar corridor, a flint was struck. The clear sound of a tinderbox being used urged action. Kit felt Iomhar's grasp around her wrist, tearing her hand from his mouth before he took her arm, tugging her away from the middle of the corridor and into one of the recesses of the red brick archways. They stood flat against the arch, side by side, arms pressed together as a candle down the corridor took light.

Kit didn't need to crane her neck around the arch to see something of what was happening, for shadows danced on the wall opposite her, revealing that whoever had walked into the cellar with this newly lit candle was wearing a vast gown with bell-shaped sleeves. The shadow looked over her shoulder, as if nervous of anyone following her down the staircase, before she tiptoed toward one of the cellar doors. Opening the door, she stepped inside, her shadow vanishing behind her.

"It's the wine cellar," Iomhar murmured in Kit's ear, coming so close that she jumped in surprise. "What was that? Ye cold?"

"Shh!" she urged once more.

Within seconds, the shadow reappeared, staring down at a wine bottle in her hands. She didn't move for a minute, but gazed at it, then glanced repeatedly over her shoulder, before hurrying to the staircase. Once the shadow was gone, along with the candle, Kit and Iomhar sighed into the darkness, leaning their heads against the wall.

"She was furtive," Kit said.

"It could have just been a lady stealing a bottle of wine, Kit."

"How many fine ladies wearing dresses like that are there in the palace right now?" she asked.

Beside her, she heard Iomhar pulling a small tinderbox from his pocket. A light was eventually struck, and the candle was lit, casting a small orange glow. The scent of burning tallow lingered under their noses.

"Only the queen's ladies," Iomhar nodded in realisation.

"Just so. Why would a wealthy lady steal a bottle of wine? One of them is behind the poisoning, I am sure of it." Kit moved off the wall, standing in the centre of the corridor.

"Ye think they intend to poison the queen again? With wine this time?"

"I think it possible." Kit stepped away, making a decision. "From now on, they will have to be watched."

# CHAPTER 12

"This is hopeless," Kit murmured as she followed Lady Hardwick back into the queen's chambers. She had followed her at a distance for most of the day, though little good it had done her. Lady Hardwick had merely visited a privy and asked how the injured staff from the explosion in the kitchen had fared, but she had gone nowhere else, nor given the slightest hint of disloyalty to the queen. At one point, Kit thought she saw Lady Hardwick hiding in a corner with her hands pressed to her eyes, trying to stop tears. When a maid passed, she immediately dropped her hands. Kit rather suspected the lady was fond of keeping up appearances.

Kit stood at the far end of the privy chamber, leaning against the window as she stared at Lady Hardwick across the room. Of all the ladies gathered there, Lady Hardwick seemed to be the most likely traitor. Had she not housed Mary Stuart in her own home? Had she not had the chance to be turned by that rhetoric?

"You are staring." Lady Hunsdon approached, with a hint of wonder in her expression. "It is not proper, you know. To stare in such a way."

"Lady Hunsdon, I am not here to impress as a lady."

"That I can tell," Lady Hunsdon said, gesturing at Kit's clothes.

"I am here to protect the queen. That requires watching people and staring. It does not require me to wear a gown or behave with propriety."

Lady Hunsdon looked away, her dark blue eyes turning to the window on which Kit was leaning. After some minutes of silence, with Lady Hunsdon making no effort to move away, Kit took the opportunity to ask questions.

"What do you know of Lady Hardwick?" she asked, nodding her head across the room. "She is a favourite of the ladies."

"Most certainly. She was a favourite of the queen's once too."

"Your words suggest it is not the case anymore," Kit murmured.

Lady Hunsdon smiled sadly. "They are friends, Miss Scarlett. They may argue, but in truth I think they both take pleasure in the argument. With the news of Lady Hardwick dividing herself from her latest husband, the queen extended the invitation for her to come and stay here. Lady Hardwick likes to pretend that nothing can hurt her, but…"

"But what?"

"I rather thought there were tears in her eyes when she saw the queen again upon her return. Perhaps that is the gratitude."

Kit chewed her lip, growing unsettled. If Lady Hardwick was indebted to the queen and had the relationship with her that had just been described, she did not seem a likely poisoner. "Tell me, Lady Hunsdon, are all the ladies allowed private access to the queen?"

"No, not all."

"Who then?"

"Lady Stafford and I, principally. Miss Parry too, and Lady Gifford."

Kit's eyes darted toward Miss Parry and Lady Gifford. Miss Parry was young, barely more than a child, and she seemed in awe of the tales Lady Hardwick was telling her. Lady Gifford, however, was distracted at this moment, looking down at her hands and fidgeting with them.

As Lady Hunsdon walked away from Kit, moving toward the withdrawing chamber to see the queen, Kit's eyes never left Lady Gifford. Soon, Lady Gifford stood and departed from the privy chamber, promising she would return. Kit waited only a minute after she had left before following her.

Lady Gifford was hastening through the corridor toward the staircase, where she passed Iomhar on the stairs. They barely nodded at one another as Lady Gifford was so much in haste. Kit increased her pace, trying to catch up with her when Iomhar met her on the landing.

"Kit, I need to speak to ye."

"Did you find the gunpowder?"

"Nay."

"Then it can wait." Kit tried to run ahead to the staircase, but Iomhar stepped in her way.

"It is important. I have just seen Walsingham. Something he said… It isn't right."

"What does that mean?" Kit asked.

"I do not know exactly." He sighed and ran a hand through his hair. "I am certain he is telling us lies."

"Iomhar, can we discuss this another time?" Kit pleaded, angling her head around his arm to look down the steps. Lady Gifford's gown was flapping at the bottom of the staircase.

"I have a question for ye. Have ye spoken to Walsingham yet?"

"About my suspicion of the ladies?" Kit asked as she tugged on Iomhar's arm, looking for where Lady Gifford had gone.

"Nay, Kit, about your dream."

She snapped her gaze toward him, her anger burning. "Iomhar, this is hardly the time for me to have that conversation with him, is it?"

"When will be the time?" Iomhar asked. "When this commission is done, there will be another, aye, will there not?"

"Iomhar, not at this moment." She turned her head, seeing Lady Gifford had vanished from the vast staircase. Muttering a curse under her breath, she darted to the window, peering down through the glass and waiting for Lady Gifford to make an appearance. Seconds later, she did, moving through the fountain courtyard and lifting the hood of a cloak over her head, hiding her face. She was walking with clear purpose.

Kit took off, heading for the stairs, but Iomhar caught her arm.

"Iomhar!"

"What are ye doing?" he asked, glancing through the window. "We are having this conversation, Kit."

"We will have it another time. I am following one of the queen's ladies." Kit managed to break free of his hold and pushed him in the chest, urging him toward the queen's chambers. "Take my place guarding the queen's door whilst I follow the lady."

"Following your orders now, am I?" he asked, a small smile appearing on his lips.

"Yes! You do not usually complain about doing so. Now go. There is no time to discuss this further."

"Then we will discuss it another time." He held her gaze for a second before hurrying off down the corridor, heading for the queen's rooms.

Kit lost no more time. She moved to the window to see Lady Gifford had reached the other end of the courtyard and had a door open. Stepping inside, her manner was furtive, peering beyond the edges of her hood and checking the courtyard to see if anyone was following her through the growing dusk. As the door closed, Kit took off, running down the steps and out through a door into the courtyard.

As she reached the cobblestone square, she sprinted across and slowed her pace when she reached the other side, opening the door as quietly as she could before stepping inside.

This part of the palace was one that was new to her. It appeared to be rooms for the staff, the corridors too narrow for a lady with a wide skirt. Far ahead, Lady Gifford was struggling through the growing darkness, having to tug harshly at her dress to bring it with her. When she reached a narrow opening, she slipped through with the silk and velvet noisily brushing against the timberwork.

Kit followed, keeping her body pressed into the shadows of the corridor. When she reached the same opening, she peered through the gap, hiding behind the frame.

It was a chamber for the staff to gather in, with a table at one end bearing empty tankards. Against a wall there was a cabinet, with the doors ajar as Lady Gifford poked her head inside. She was feeling around for something, her hands knocking against the wood. She even squealed in irritation, before her hand slowly pulled something out of the cabinet.

In the dim light, Kit could just about see what was in her clutches. It was a small glass vial, pale blue in colour with a tiny cork stoppering the top. As Lady Gifford held the vial up for inspection, her young lips curling into a smile, her expression chilled Kit to the bone. She was taking delight in the glass vial, as if whatever was inside could be the answer to her prayers. From under her cloak, she retrieved a bottle — the same sort of bottle that Kit had seen taken from the wine cellar earlier that day. Lady Gifford decanted the blue vial into the bottle, then shook it up before corking it and returning the vial to the cabinet.

"Hail Mary, full of grace." The muttered words made Kit stand taller as she recognised the Catholic prayer. Lady Gifford then closed her eyes and crossed herself.

Kit backed up, hurrying from the archway and walking down the corridor, moving soundlessly on the balls of her feet. As soon as she found an open doorway, she stepped inside, pressing herself close to the door and waiting for Lady Gifford to come past. The lady soon did, stuffing the glass bottle up her bell-shaped sleeve before rushing down the corridor.

Once Kit heard the closing of the door, she stepped out from her hiding place, hurrying into the courtyard. She was careful to leave a gap between her and Lady Gifford, though she kept her in view. They traipsed through the courtyard and back into the main rooms, passing through the great hall and up the staircase in the direction of the queen's chambers. The closer they moved to the rooms, the faster Lady Gifford seemed to walk.

Reaching the corridor outside of the privy chamber, Kit hovered on the staircase, peering over the top step to watch Lady Gifford be permitted inside, passing the gentleman-at-arms and Iomhar, who stood guard. Once the door closed, Kit sprinted down the corridor to reach them. Iomhar's gaze flicked toward her.

"Aye, what is it?" he asked knowingly as she reached his side. "What has happened?"

"I think it has yet to happen. Be on your guard." She gestured to his weapons' belt. "Come if I call for you."

He nodded and opened the door for her, hurrying her inside. As Kit stepped in, she found the ladies-in-waiting in various positions of repose. Lady Hardwick was calling her friend.

"Lady Gifford, come, sit with me a while. I was telling Miss Radcliff and Miss Parry about the young days between the queen and myself. Would you not like to hear them?"

"Soon, my lady. If Lady Hunsdon permits it, I would like to see how Her Majesty is faring?" Lady Gifford turned to Lady Hunsdon, who had stepped in from the withdrawing chamber. Her wide face was tired, with heavy shadows under her eyes. She nodded and yawned.

"Of course," she said quietly. "Urge Dorothy to retire too, if you can. She will scarcely leave the queen's side. She needs rest, as we all do." Lady Hunsdon sat in a chair by the door, placing a hand to her chest.

Lady Gifford nodded and entered the withdrawing chamber.

Kit paused, not wanting to follow straight away. She wished to give Lady Gifford a chance to prove her guilt, so she walked to Lady Hunsdon's side and bent down beside her.

"I do not have the energy for our usual bitter conversations." Lady Hunsdon waved a hand toward her dismissively. "Had you done your task better, my queen would not be dying."

"Then I will be brief," Kit whispered. "In a minute, I may call for help from the gentlemen at that door. I beg you, my lady, do not stop them. Their appearance could be the thing that saves the queen."

Lady Hunsdon said nothing, but she nodded once, making it plain she would not argue against such a thing.

The sound of footsteps prompted Kit to stand and turn to the door of the withdrawing chamber. Lady Stafford appeared, as bleary-eyed as Lady Hunsdon was, leaning on the doorframe. Kit urged her out with an impatient gesture of her hand.

"What is it?" Lady Stafford asked.

"Shh," Kit pleaded, stepping forward again. She had now caught the attention of all the ladies in the room, even Lady Hardwick and Miss Parry, who broke off from their conversation and sat forward.

"Not a word, ladies," Lady Hunsdon whispered.

Kit nodded to her, thanking her for the momentary belief. With Lady Stafford stepping to the side, Kit placed a hand on her weapons' belt, reaching for the hilt of one of her daggers and pulling it out of its scabbard. Miss Radcliff let out a small squeal at the sight, until Lady Hardwick slapped her arm.

Kit crept through the withdrawing chamber, inching toward the netted curtain. When she reached it, she watched as the shadowy figure of Lady Gifford came into view.

She was beside the queen, who laid on the bed, her gaunt figure lit by three candles. Lady Gifford reached into her sleeve and pulled out the short bottle she had taken from the cellar. Slowly, she poured out a little wine into a spindly crystal glass, swilling the contents around.

As she moved to sit on the edge of the bed, reaching to place the glass to the queen's lips, Kit lifted the net curtain. Without making a sound, she stepped into the room.

"Your Majesty, it is a new tonic from the apothecary. You must drink," Lady Gifford pleaded. With one hand, she urged the queen to sit up a little. The queen strained on her pillows, the sinews in her neck plain to see, thin and string-like as she reached up toward the glass.

The crystal was a finger's breadth away from those greyish lips when Kit stepped behind Lady Gifford, pulling her dagger forward and placing it across the lady's throat.

"Do not move," she whispered.

The queen's eyes shot open, widening when she saw Lady Gifford and Kit above her. Lady Gifford tried to push the glass forward one more time, but Kit lashed out, taking hold of the lady's hair and dragging her back with her free hand. Lady Gifford squeaked and dropped the glass. Red wine spilled across the queen's bedsheets, trickling like blood on either side of her body.

"Iomhar!" Kit bellowed.

Doors burst open, followed by the panicked cries of the ladies-in-waiting. Seconds later, the net was lifted and Iomhar tumbled into the room with the gentleman-at-arms by his side. Kit dragged Lady Gifford off the bed and forced her to her knees on the floor.

"We have our poisoner."

# CHAPTER 13

"Tell me!" Walsingham roared.

Kit looked away, unable to bear the sight. She turned to the yellow wall of the dungeon, the stonework glistening in the torchlight. Just as Walsingham's bellowed orders bounced off the arched stone ceiling that was far above them, so did the cries of Lady Gifford.

"This isn't right," Iomhar muttered at Kit's side. "She will say anything to stop the pain."

"I heard that, Iomhar." Walsingham's voice was firm.

"Aye, which is a good thing then."

Kit turned round, leaning against the wall beside Iomhar to face the sight once more. Lady Gifford was in the centre of the cell, her dress muddied from the stone floor and her hands red and scorched from where they had made her hold the hot poker. A gloved gaoler took the poker back, adding it to the fire on the other side of the dungeon, where the metal glowed red once again.

"Torture does no good," Kit whispered, her eyes falling on Lady Gifford.

"I will be the judge of that." Walsingham stood tall as he spoke. For a minute, he appeared as the younger man Kit could remember from when she was a child. She saw no weakness in him, no sign of the sickness she knew plagued his bones. It seemed he was unwilling to show that vulnerability to their prisoner. "How many times did you poison the queen?" Walsingham asked.

Lady Gifford lifted her chin off her chest, holding out her burnt hands with the fingers curled, trembling madly. Her eyes appeared darker than usual, almost dead.

"Two or three times," Kit answered before Lady Gifford could.

"Three," Lady Gifford confirmed. Kit nodded; there had to be the first poisoning to result in the queen taking to her bed, administered via her makeup. Then there was the addition to the apothecary's tonic, and she could have easily drunk that more than once.

"Why? Why did you do it?" Walsingham barked, bending down with his hands on his knees. Lady Gifford said nothing, hanging her head forward. "Bring the poker back." He beckoned to the gaoler to collect the metal again.

"No!" Lady Gifford panicked, leaning away in her chair.

"She is a Catholic." Kit walked up to stand behind Lady Gifford, catching Walsingham's eye. He held up his hand, stopping the gaoler from bringing the poker any further forward.

"You are certain, Kit?"

"Yes." Kit nodded. "The Catholic Queen of Scots on the throne would be infinitely preferable to Lady Gifford, would it not be?"

"Is it true?" Walsingham turned his gaze down to Lady Gifford. "Say it now, if you wish to keep the skin on your hands. Was this your aim?"

"No more, I beg you, no more." She tried to hide her hands in the dirtied folds of her gown, but the gaoler advanced, bearing the poker another time.

"Say it! Now."

"Enough." Kit stepped around Lady Gifford, her movement so sudden that Walsingham stepped back, his chin tilting downward. "You do not give her time to answer you. She is too busy pleading with you not to hurt her again."

"This is not your place, Kit."

"It is my place to work for you and get answers, even when your methods of finding those answers are maniacal."

"Maniacal?" Walsingham spluttered, spittle appearing at the corners of his lips.

"Away." Kit gestured to the gaoler, forcing him to back up before she took Walsingham's place. Rather than standing over Lady Gifford, she knelt down on the floor, catching the woman's eye. "Someone left the poison in that servant's room for you to collect, did they not?"

Lady Gifford's lips began to tremble.

"Who left it there for you to find?"

"They did not give me a name," Lady Gifford whispered. Walsingham and Iomhar stepped forward to hear her. Kit shot them a silent warning with her eyes, urging them not to come too close.

"Did they give you anything? A place name? A code?" Kit pleaded.

"An emblem." Lady Gifford's voice shook.

"What emblem?" Kit asked softly. Lady Gifford tried to bend over her hands, cowering to protect them, but she squealed at the pain all the more. "What emblem, Lady Gifford?"

The sound of the poker scraping in the fire showed that the gaoler was thinking of using it again. Kit held up a hand toward him.

"A unicorn." Lady Gifford's words made Kit sit back on her knees, knowing the meaning. She looked up to Iomhar, seeing the same realisation on his face.

"Do you know the name Lord Ruskin?" Kit asked, spinning back to look at Lady Gifford.

"I know the name." She nodded slowly, her lips trembling all the more. "I heard it, once."

"From whom?"

She shook her head, clearly having no intention of saying the words.

"The explosion in the kitchen. Did you know it was going to happen?"

Lady Gifford slowly nodded, refusing to meet Kit's gaze.

"Do you know of another? Another explosion?"

"I do not know when, but … they said it would happen."

"Who? Who said it would happen? Lord Ruskin?"

"The letter. No name. No code. Just a letter." Lady Gifford shook her head. "My husband gave me the letter. The letter told me of the explosion and gave me my instructions for what to do."

"Lord Gifford," Walsingham spat across the room in anger. "He is still Catholic after all. I knew it."

Kit shot one look in his direction, pleading with him to be quiet. He acquiesced, leaning against the wall beside the gaoler and returning his glare to the fire.

"Did they give you your orders for the poisoning in the letter?" Kit asked, earning another nod from Lady Gifford. "What do they call you in the letter, Lady Gifford? What codename do they give you? No one writes a letter with a real name these days, in case it is found."

Lady Gifford lifted a hand, staring at the white blistered line that ran through her palm from the poker. "The Lily."

Kit almost fell over as she twisted on the spot, turning to look at Iomhar. He was shaking his head.

"Nay. Luca said they were both men, close to the queen."

"He only knew who one was," Kit whispered. "He didn't know who the other was. He may have presumed the Lily was a man."

"What are you two muttering about?" Walsingham asked, stepping forward.

"Luca suggested there were two men close to the queen who supported a plot to overthrow her and march an army on London, with Mary Stuart at the head. They have codenames. One of them was the Lily," Kit explained as she stood. Walsingham cursed, remembering what she had told him when she and Iomhar had returned from Northumberland. She shifted her focus to Lady Gifford. "Who is behind the gunpowder, Lady Gifford? Do they call themselves the Rose?"

"I do not know."

"Yet you know it is happening. There must be something else you know, anything."

"What of Lord Ruskin?" Iomhar asked, stepping forward. "Luca claimed Ruskin knew both the Rose and the Lily. My lady, is Lord Ruskin behind the gunpowder?"

She looked up, meeting his gaze as tears began to trickle out of her eyes. "I thought he was in Scotland," she whispered. "Please…" She reached up to Kit, grasping her doublet before crying out at the pain in her hands, though she didn't let go. "No more. I beg you, do not let them do it again."

Kit slowly placed her hand over Lady Gifford's knuckles, urging her to release her. "This is over," she said, turning to Walsingham.

"I say when it is over, Kit."

"She has told you what she knows. All you will be doing is hurting a woman who has nothing left to give you." Kit backed away, sensing Iomhar following her out of the room.

She took hold of the iron door, swinging it open and stumbling into the stone corridor. Iomhar closed the door behind them as Kit placed a hand to her mouth, feeling the nausea begin to settle.

"Did you see her hands?" she whispered in horror.

"Aye. I hope Walsingham listens to ye. I cannot bear to hear those shouts again." He shook his head and gestured for her to keep walking. "We have the Lily, Kit."

"If the Lily was behind the poisoning, then surely the Rose is responsible for the gunpowder."

"Or Lord Ruskin."

"What?" Kit stopped by a thin staircase, turning to face him in the darkness. "She said he was in Scotland."

"Nay, Kit. She said she *thought* he was in Scotland. Aye, she was veiling the fact she did not know, not for certain. For all we know, Lord Ruskin could be anywhere, even in London."

"He could have been the man I saw in the garden, wearing that cloak."

"Aye, he could."

Kit hurried down the staircase, with Iomhar following. "I need a drink."

"Aye, me too. Find the gaolers' rooms; they'll have something."

"Ye must speak to Walsingham about your dreams," Iomhar said as they stepped out of the Tower of London a short while later, having refreshed themselves.

"Why is it so important to you that I do this now?" Kit asked. Night was thick around them. The only light cascaded from the orange torches that burned against the Tower's walls.

Iomhar's jaw tightened. "It is something that Walsingham said earlier today. When I told him that our latest search for the gunpowder was fruitless…" He paused. "It was strange." He lowered his voice, taking her arm and leading her further away from the Tower.

"Do you truly believe someone is listening to us out here?" Kit laughed.

"He is a spymaster, Kit. Do not forget that." His whisper grew more urgent as they stepped away from the Tower, disappearing into a side lane that was so dark, Kit could only see Iomhar's outline. "I asked him if there were more cellars or tunnels of any kind at Hampton Court, perhaps from the Thames. There has to be another place this gunpowder is hidden. He talked of a small chamber, accessible from the river at low tide. Too small for me to climb into. When I suggested ye could search it, he shook his head. He muttered something about ye not being good with deep water."

Kit stopped walking and Iomhar halted beside her.

"Aye, I know."

"I have never told him I was afraid of water."

"Am I the only one ye have ever told? Aye, I feel blessed indeed. Ye trusted me with a secret."

"Of course I did," Kit said dismissively, finding that the words came easily in the darkness, now that she could not see his face. "I tell you many secrets, it seems."

"Aye. It is a trust returned, Kit." His voice was closer than she had expected, and she stepped away. He cleared his throat. "Could he have seen ye were afraid of water as a child?"

Kit didn't answer straight away. She chewed her lip, trying to think of the moments she had shared with Walsingham. "I avoided water, at all costs. I did not want him to know."

"Ye hid it from him? All those years?"

"I thought I had. I did not want him to think less of me." She snatched off her hat, wringing it in her hands as she thought back to when she was very young. "Wait…" She came to a stop, so abruptly that Iomhar collided with her in the darkness.

"Kit? What is it?"

"I…" She trailed off, trying to put it into words. The feeling was easy to recall, but the words Walsingham had actually used were much harder to remember. She had been standing by a pond on the Barn Elms estate, a little older than when she had first come to him. Walsingham and his wife had been there, with his wife carrying Franny when she was just a baby. Walsingham had walked alongside Kit, pointing to the pond and gesturing to the fish.

"Kit?" Iomhar urged, his hand still on her back, trying to coax an answer out of her.

"The pond at Barn Elms. Walsingham was trying to tell me the names of the fish."

"He was?" Iomhar's voice had darkened. "For some reason, I find it difficult to imagine that man being like a father to ye."

Kit shifted at his words. She had never considered Walsingham to be a father. He was the man that watched over her, a guardian of some kind, that was all.

"I did not like the water; I scrambled back from it. He took my hand and led me away."

"So, he noticed ye were afraid of water?"

"No, Iomhar, it was what he said." She angled her head, trying to look behind her, though it was too dark to see Iomhar's expression. "He said, 'I know.'"

"I know what?" Iomhar asked.

"'I know, Kitty, I know. You do not have to go in the water again.'"

Iomhar's palm dropped from her back, and he reached for her hand, pulling her in the direction from which they had come.

"Where are we going?"

"Back to the Tower. Do ye really need any more proof that your dream is a memory, Kit? Ye need to ask him of it."

"Not now." She pulled on his hand, jerking him to a stop in the middle of the road.

"Then when?" Iomhar asked impatiently.

"When this is over. I give you my word, Iomhar. I will ask him then."

He breathed deeply as he whipped round to face her, his body close to hers. "Your word?" he murmured.

"Yes. But not now, not tonight."

"Aye, very well." Iomhar continued down the road, towing Kit behind him. She made no effort to pull her hand out of his, still thinking of the incident by the pond. "We need some rest before the morning. We will be on duty with the sunrise."

"The gunpowder," Kit whispered. "Where else do we look?"

"I have a few ideas."

They crossed into a street, inching nearer to Kit's lodgings. As they walked, clouds parted to reveal the moon, bathing the streets in a thin white light. Kit lifted her chin, now able to see there was a figure standing outside the door to her lodgings. The fact that someone had been in her rooms was still stark in her mind. She tugged Iomhar to a stop, not letting him see the figure in the doorway.

"What is it?"

"Your house is closer to the palace," she said hurriedly, leading him down a lane far away from her road. With just one glance, she saw the shadowy figure in the doorway step forward. He had clearly been waiting for her.

"Aye, it is," Iomhar said. "Any reason ye do not wish to sleep in your own lodgings? Would it have anything to do with that dodgy lock on your door?"

"Perhaps I feel sorry for you in that big empty house, as you call it." Kit encouraged him to walk faster, and Iomhar obliged. "You have enough spare chambers, do you not?"

"Plenty."

Every now and then she glanced back to see if they were being followed, though Iomhar appeared not to notice. Once or twice, she thought she saw a shadow moving, but then it vanished, making her doubt that there was anyone there at all. The figure in the doorway confirmed one thing for her, however. Whoever had followed her from Hampton Court that day and searched her rooms was not done yet. They were waiting for her to appear again.

# CHAPTER 14

"It is abundantly clear you need the help," Kit said to Iomhar the next morning.

"I am not so incapable of doing my job without ye."

"Have you found the gunpowder yet?"

Iomhar didn't answer as the cart pulled up the driveway.

Kit leaned across, elbowing him in the side. "You merely do not wish to admit that you need help," she said, taking delight in the way Iomhar was squirming and trying to avoid looking at her. He kept his attention on the drive, watching the staff that were ambling back and forth across the palace estate. "So? What is your answer?"

Iomhar sighed and turned his green eyes on her. "Aye, very well. Help me, Kit. I only have a few ideas left of where to look for the gunpowder."

The sound of another cart pulling up prompted them both to turn back to the drive. This cart was arriving much more quickly than their own, ridden with a kind of wildness. As the driver pulled on the reins, forcing the horse to come to a stop, the steed reared, frustrated at being manhandled so. The figure on the cart leapt down, stumbling slightly and then standing straight. Kit recognised the face of Walsingham hurrying toward them.

"Walsingham?" she called. His face was stern, his beady gaze unblinking. "What has happened?"

"She has gone."

"Gone?" Kit repeated, knowing exactly what Walsingham meant without any further explanation. "The Tower of London was broken into?"

"That I do not know." He came to a stop before Kit and Iomhar, his fists shaking with rage. "I went to see Lady Gifford first thing this morning. The gaolers had found her cell unlocked, the key still in the door, and she was gone."

Kit stood still, watching as Walsingham looked between them.

"Do you not realise what this does to us? Whoever has placed that gunpowder here now has an ally free, ready to warn him that we know of it." He waved toward them madly. "You have to find it! At once, before her ally can panic. This Rose, Lord Ruskin or whoever he may be that has put the powder here. We must find it before it can be lit. The two of you, go. Now!"

Kit and Iomhar backed up, turning into the courtyard under the gatehouse. Kit's mind was still processing exactly what had happened when Iomhar called a meeting with the yeomen and the other intelligencers that had been placed in Hampton Court's walls. He gave quick orders, demanding they checked every nook they had already searched once. They were not to leave a vessel unopened, nor a lid down. When the yeomen divided off, each one running to their post, Iomhar crossed the courtyard, heading back out of the palace walls.

"Where are you going?" Kit called, following him. They rounded the outer walls, where Iomhar jumped up on a low boundary, standing astride it as he stared down at the Thames nearby. The river curved alongside the lawn that sat beside the palace. Kit leapt up behind him, remembering what he had said the night before about a chamber beneath the palace, accessible at low tide. "No one would place the gunpowder in a chamber that floods, Iomhar. It would hardly dry out enough to be usable."

"Aye, true. Yet who says there is only one chamber down there?" he asked, turning to look at her with raised eyebrows. "What if there is more than one chamber, and the first is the only one that floods?"

"Did Walsingham say as much?"

"Nay, he said he has never seen it beyond the tiny opening. He heard it whispered of once in King Edward's court. That is all."

Kit shifted and looked down at the water that was seeping backward with low tide quickly approaching. "I wonder why you asked for my help after all?" she said wryly as she leapt down to the other side of the wall, walking toward the river.

"I won't stay far back."

"Some use that will be, if I am the only one who will fit in there."

"The tide is far enough out now," Iomhar declared after they had waited some minutes and clambered down off the bank, landing on the silted riverbed. Kit did not follow straight away. She was still eyeing the retreating water with caution, watching as thin trickles raised up around Iomhar's boots then settled down again. "Trust me, Kit."

She hastened down the bank, following closely behind him and never taking her eyes off the water.

"Where is this chamber?" she asked distractedly.

"There." He lifted a hand and pointed ahead. Kit tore her gaze from the water and looked round, seeing a patch of darkness in the rocks at the side of the riverbed.

"Is that an opening? It looks more like a shadow."

"Aye, little more than a cave." Iomhar led the way. When he bent down and peered in through the gap, Kit cursed.

"God's blood, you wish for me to fit in there? You need a child for that!"

"Ye can go on your hands and knees." He gestured at the earth. Kit cursed again, looking from the water to the opening. She could see nothing but darkness. "I would do it if I could," Iomhar added.

"I can do it." Kit waved Iomhar back and then dropped to her knees. "Shout to me if the tide comes in."

He smiled teasingly. "Ye didn't think I was just going to leave ye in there, did ye?"

She smiled back before clambering forward into the opening. It grew even narrower at one point, forcing her to slide forward on her stomach, catching her doublet on the rocks. When the ground dropped away in front of her, she practically fell into a chamber.

She had to blink a few times as she stood, adjusting to the darkness. The room was empty, and barely wide enough to accommodate the span of her arms. What was clear was the extent of the flooding, with some water still splashing around her ankles.

"Anything?" Iomhar called to her.

"Nothing." She turned around in the chamber, her eyes landing on the wall ahead of her. It was not stonework, nor earth, but boards that had been slatted together, as if intended to keep out the water from her side.

"Iomhar?" Kit called through the thin opening.

"Aye?"

"I think there is another chamber. It has been boarded up."

"Boarded? How big?"

Kit stepped closer to the opening, trying to determine how far the boarding stretched through the darkened room. It was hard to tell what the room had originally been intended for when the palace was built. Perhaps another cellar for wine or ale, which was quickly discovered to flood and abandoned. Grasping one of the boards, she lifted herself up, looking through a narrow gap above a plank to find there was a room beyond, one that was not as dark as where she stood. There was a candle inside it, the flame flickering.

Kit dropped down once more, looking at the boards in front of her. They were old, clearly boarded up years ago, and lifted at an angle to her, so that when the room where she stood would flood at high tide, it would not seep through the boards into the second chamber. The boards were too old-looking to have been placed there recently, but they were still intact. In confusion, Kit took hold of them again, lifting herself up enough to peer through the gap.

That candle continued to flicker. Around it, she could not see enough to be certain what the room was, but there was something beneath a sheet, something undisturbed.

Stumbling away from the boards, Kit reached toward the thin opening once more.

"Kit?"

"I'm coming out," she called to Iomhar, scrambling through the space on her hands and knees. On the other side Iomhar helped her out, taking her hand to help her up.

"Ye seem panicked."

"I am." She stumbled away from him, heading further back along the sediment of the riverbed and angling her face up to the palace walls on the other side. "What room is that?"

"Where?"

"There." She pointed straight above them. "Within the palace wall. What room is that?"

"Guest chambers, that is all."

"Empty?" Kit said. She had an idea, one that might give them a result at last.

"Aye."

"They are not empty, Iomhar." She took off back across the riverbed, her feet sloshing through the mud as she clambered toward the grassy bank.

"What do ye mean they are not? Kit, we have searched them all, more than once." He followed her, jumping up onto the bank as she reached for the wall.

"Then there is a room there that has not been searched. Did you find a cellar?" she asked, clambering onto the wall and turning back to face Iomhar momentarily. The empty look on his face made her pause. "No? You did not find a cellar?"

"There isn't one in that part of the house. Only in the kitchens."

"There is, Iomhar. I saw it." She jumped down on the other side of the wall, beckoning him to follow.

They pushed past the yeomen at the gate with such speed that they all jumped to attention, loudly asking what the great fuss was. Kit didn't bother to answer them; she merely kept running to the guest quarters and through a door at the far side of the base courtyard. She then ran along the corridor, shoving open each door in turn and peering in, looking for any sign of a cellar.

"Kit?" Iomhar called behind her.

"There is a cellar somewhere," she shouted back to him. "I saw it, Iomhar. Beyond the boarding. There is another room with a lit candle inside."

"I searched these rooms myself. There is nay doorway to a cellar."

Kit stopped walking as she reached the end of the corridor, pushing her hands into her hair in frustration. If there was no doorway then it had to be hidden, somewhere that was not easy to find.

"If a room is disused, what happens to it?" she asked Iomhar. "It is boarded up, yes?"

"Aye, or the doorway is blocked off. Hidden."

"Then look for a door that cannot be found." She pushed into the room beside her, walking around the bed and the furniture. She started with the walls, knocking and listening for any hollow sound.

Iomhar walked along the floorboards and stamped on each one, checking whether any were loose.

The first room yielded nothing, and they moved on to the second. Kit found nothing in the walls, but as Iomhar stamped on the floorboards something eventually cracked beneath his foot. Kit spun round. Iomhar had half a floorboard in his hand, for it had flicked up in the air.

He bent down hurriedly and lifted more floorboards. Kit moved to his side, peering over his shoulder to see a thin flight of steps that reached down into the ground. One side was flanked by a grey stone wall, mossy and green with mould. The other side was made out of earth, curving as if in danger of falling in on the stairs at any second.

"Nay wonder they boarded it up," Iomhar murmured, tossing the last of the floorboards to the side. "This could come down any minute." He gestured to the bank of earth.

"I am willing to risk it." Kit practically jumped past him in her eagerness to get down the steps. They were wet, forcing her to grab on to the wall to stop herself from falling, as Iomhar followed.

When she reached the bottom of the staircase, the ground stretched out before her, made of flagstones. She had to bend to avoid hitting her head on a low timber beam, stepping through an archway into a chamber where a candle flickered ahead. She came to a stop, recognising the room she had observed from the chamber beneath the river.

The same candle was before her, standing tall on a wrought-iron stand. The tallow was burning down quickly. The light from its flame wouldn't last much longer.

"What is this place?" Iomhar murmured.

"The other side of those boards." Kit gestured ahead to a wall made of boarding. Along the bottom edge, sandbags had been placed, warding off leaks.

Iomhar stepped forward, moving toward a lump under a grey sheet covering. Slowly, he reached for it.

"What are you waiting for?" Kit murmured.

"I am thinking of two things." He looked to her, his hand still hovering. "First, as that candle is lit, whoever lit it is not distant from us. Second, do ye have anything on ye that can make a spark?"

She gestured down at the daggers in her belt, as he looked at the pistol and the sword in his.

"Do not let them touch, aye? We cannot have a spark."

"Aye," she echoed, prompting him to smile a little before he lifted the cover. Kit stepped back into the shadows as five barrels were revealed. These were taller and narrower than ale barrels, each one not bound with iron but with rope. "Is it…?" Kit trailed off as Iomhar lifted the lid of the first barrel.

"Aye, it's gunpowder."

She stepped forward, peering into the barrel to see the black powder.

"Put out the flame. Now. We can't risk it being lit."

Kit stepped forward, blowing out the candle. She saw a brief smoke trail before they were cast into darkness so thick that it could have been the depths of night. "Well, that was a good idea," she murmured, feeling around.

"We cannot risk it going off." Iomhar was insistent, his voice getting nearer to her.

"Ow, that was my foot."

"Well, I can hardly see your foot, can I?" Iomhar asked.

There was a tap somewhere behind them.

"Shh!" Kit urged. She could hear Iomhar murmuring something. She reached out, making a grab for his arm to stop him speaking, and instead made contact with his weapons belt.

"Is there a reason ye have such a tight hold of me?"

"Do not say another word," she whispered, leaning up toward him. He fell silent as there was another tap.

Kit looked round, back toward the timber beam and the bottom of the stairs, realising that the tap was a footstep on the staircase. She inched away from Iomhar, moving back toward the stairs, wanting a look at whoever had followed them.

The closer she moved, the more the stairs came into view, with light filtering down from the room above. The stranger's feet appeared first, in long boots that reached up his calves. Next came a yeoman's clothes. He reached the bottom of the stairs, looking up and tilting his hat back to reveal his face.

The fair hair, the pale blue eyes and the wan complexion were all familiar to her. She may have only seen him once before on the coast of Northumberland, but she had committed that face to memory.

It was Lord Ruskin.

# CHAPTER 15

"Iomhar," Kit whispered, pulling at his arm as Lord Ruskin stepped forward.

"Shadows in the cellar, what may they be?" Lord Ruskin said with humour in his tone as he struck a light, trying to see the two of them better. He stepped further into the cellar, reaching for the tallow candle they had just put out and lighting it again. Kit inched forward, longing to put it out with one blow, but Lord Ruskin held the flame over the gunpowder barrels, warning her not to come any closer. "Miss Scarlett, still as poorly dressed as ever, I see," he chuckled before his eyes turned to Iomhar.

Kit watched the expression change in an instant. The skin around his eyes quivered, as if he couldn't believe what he was seeing. Iomhar hadn't yet said a word, though she felt how still he had become. She was aware that he believed that Lord Ruskin knew who had been responsible for the death of his father.

"Mr Iomhar Blackwood," Lord Ruskin exclaimed, his voice high. "Ye look more like your father these days."

Kit felt Iomhar move from behind her. He reached around her with his hand outstretched, as if threatening to take Lord Ruskin by the throat.

"Nay further!" Lord Ruskin warned, pulling out a pistol and pointing it in Iomhar's direction.

Kit and Iomhar froze, neither of them wanting to tempt a shot in a room full of gunpowder.

"Ye are responsible for this," Iomhar said darkly, gesturing to the powder. "This is your plan? Kill the queen and those around her in one explosion?"

"It has impact," Lord Ruskin said with a smile. "Drama, don't ye think? They will talk of it as the spark of a revolution."

"Or the end of a golden age." Kit shuddered at the delight he took in his own words. "Are you the one who wrote to Lady Gifford? Giving her the instructions for the poisoning?" she asked, watching as Lord Ruskin struggled to move his eyes to her, preferring to keep them on Iomhar.

It suddenly made sense to her. Even if the queen did not die of the poison, she would be in no state to be moved, leaving her vulnerable to the explosion. What was more, if the poisoner was caught, Lady Gifford was the one who would be punished. Lord Ruskin had sacrificed his Lily to protect himself.

"Ye have been busy asking questions." He flicked his eyes to Kit once, before looking back to Iomhar.

"What happens now?" Iomhar asked, holding his hands outward. "Make a move to light that powder, and we will stop ye."

"Have ye not seen this?" Lord Ruskin asked, waving the pistol. "I may not be the best shot, but I think even I could hit ye at this distance."

With his other hand, Lord Ruskin unwound a stretch of rope Kit had not seen before. One end of it was tied to the barrels, with the other end having been coiled up on the floor like a snake. He unwound it quickly and tossed the free end toward the staircase, evidently preparing to light it and make his escape.

"You could not escape from here in time," Kit murmured, looking between the length of rope and the five barrels. "Even if you ran and met no resistance from us, you would die here along with us all."

"Then I die in the name of my queen. It sounds rather romantic, does it not?" Lord Ruskin's pride made Kit's shoulders slump. He was passionately devoted to Mary Stuart, it seemed, so much so that his own death did not worry him, as long as it put her on the throne of England.

"Enough." Iomhar spoke once more, his voice deeper than Kit had ever heard it. "Ye can only fire one shot at a time, Ruskin. Ye know as well as I that whichever of us ye shoot, the other one will come after ye. We will stop ye."

"Then I suppose I should put the bullet where it will cause ye the most damage. Judging by the way ye are trying to shield your friend, I know where to put it." Lord Ruskin's lip curled as he shifted the barrel of the gun toward Kit, aiming straight at her head. His finger lifted to the trigger. "Goodbye, Miss Scarlett."

"The spark will kill us all!" Kit roared as Iomhar dived forward, seeing the problem at the same moment she did. The spark from the pistol going off could be enough to light all the gunpowder in that room. Not only would they be killed, but Hampton Court would be blown up, with the people inside burnt to cinders.

Iomhar tackled Lord Ruskin, taking hold of the pistol and snatching it away from him. Lord Ruskin bellowed in pain as his hand was bent backwards, forcing him to release the weapon. His other hand reached for a rapier in his belt, swinging it through the air.

He sliced it across Iomhar's back, cutting through the doublet and forcing Iomhar against the wall. He kept the pistol between him and the stonework, stopping Lord Ruskin from reaching for it again.

Kit kicked away the rope that connected the barrels together, far from Lord Ruskin's grasp. Reaching for her daggers, she was barely prepared when Lord Ruskin marched toward her, lifting the rapier.

She narrowly stopped the blade from coming down across her neck by thrusting the two daggers upward, blocking the sword. It was a challenge of strength, with Lord Ruskin winning, pushing Kit back so that her boots scraped the stones beneath her feet.

"Ye are what she saw last." Lord Ruskin seethed, spittle around his greyish lips. "Ye killed her."

Kit bristled at the accusation. "Your wife killed herself!" she snapped, to little effect.

The year before Lady Ruskin had waged a coup against Queen Elizabeth. Having planted gunpowder on a barge in the Thames, she hoped the queen would plunge to the depths of the river along with many of her councillors, before Scottish soldiers, loyal to Mary Stuart's cause, would advance from the border to seize control. Kit had been the one to pull the queen from the river's depths, before any harm could befall her. When she had pursued Lady Ruskin through the streets of London for her crimes, the woman had refused to be taken.

The memory of Lady Ruskin thrusting the dagger into her own stomach was a moment Kit could never change. It had happened too fast, Lady Ruskin alive and shouting one minute, then prostrate on the floor the next, her eyes glacial.

"For her. This is for her," Lord Ruskin spat.

"No!" Kit panicked, realising that his other hand was pulling a basilard from his belt. He lashed out toward her stomach, forcing Kit to thrust away from him, missing the scrape of the blade against her doublet by a hair's breadth.

She backed up, colliding with one of the gunpowder barrels. As it teetered, she looked to it, keeping her daggers lifted in the air, terrified of a spark. With this distraction, she was not prepared for the cut across her wrist. She yelped at the pain, swinging back round to find one of the daggers falling from her hand. It clattered to the floor, and she kicked it away, far from the gunpowder. The blood glistened across the back of her hand.

Lord Ruskin pushed her other blade away with the basilard and pushed forward, the rapier ready to cut her. Kit reached out, desperate to stop the inevitable when something appeared in front of her. The shadows confused her, making it impossible to recognise what the mass was, until she heard the grunt of agony.

"Iomhar," Kit whispered, noting his dark hair and his shoulders slumping in front of her. He was buckling forward in pain. "No…"

Lord Ruskin pulled the rapier free and stumbled away, looking down at Iomhar with a smirk.

"No!" Kit cried, louder this time as she took hold of Iomhar's back, desperately trying to keep him standing. She was not strong enough as he dropped to the floor, almost taking her with him. She stood over him, pulling at the collar of his doublet, trying to urge him to his feet, but his eyes were narrowed in pain and his teeth were gritted.

"Stop, Kit," he pleaded through the growl.

"Goodbye, Miss Scarlett." Lord Ruskin's voice snapped her attention to the other side of the cellar. Lord Ruskin had a spill in his hand. He lit the candle, then tossed the spill to the floor, the flame landing perfectly on the thin rope that was wrapped around the barrels.

"Kit, quick!" Iomhar's voice was high with fear.

Kit released him, darting forward, going straight for the rope. This gave Lord Ruskin time to escape. He turned and fled up the stairs, disappearing so fast that Kit didn't even think about following him. She reached for the flame on the rope instead, trying to snuff it out with a stamp of her foot, but it moved along, one part of the rope burning as fast as the next. Iomhar grunted nearby, desperately trying to roll over onto his knees.

"Dagger," he called to her.

Kit needed no more instruction. She jumped closer to the barrels and lifted a part of the rope that wasn't yet singed, cutting through with the blade and stopping the flame from reaching the barrels. Once done, she snatched off her hat and thrust it over the flame, snuffing it out instantly with the smell of burnt fabric filling the air.

Iomhar sighed as he fell back down to the floor. Kit scrambled toward him on her hands and knees.

"Kit … Ruskin…" He pointed toward the stairs where Lord Ruskin had fled, struggling for words.

"You think I can go after him now?" she scoffed in fear, looking down at his stomach. The cloak had been sliced clean through, as had the dark green doublet. Lord Ruskin had clearly stabbed straight through his side.

The sight of the blood made bile rise in Kit's throat.

"How bad?" Iomhar whispered, his voice growing weaker.

She couldn't answer. She placed the doublet and the cloak tightly over his stomach and reached for his belt, shifting it higher to hold the wound closed.

"Brace yourself." As she tightened the belt, Iomhar grunted loudly, like an animal shot with a crossbow as his body stiffened beneath her.

"How much blood, Kit? How much blood?" he asked impatiently.

There were red puddles in her palms. It was leaking down his side too, pooling in the cobbles and circling the bottom of the barrels.

"Not much," she lied.

"Ye are a bad liar." His eyes closed.

"Iomhar? No. You have to stay awake." She shook his shoulders, but he didn't appear to hear her. His eyes fluttered open for a second before closing. "No! Wake up!" she bellowed in his ear, yet it did nothing.

The sight of Iomhar unmoving with his hand loosening from around the pistol he had taken from Lord Ruskin urged her into action. She released him, jumping to her feet and running up the stairs of the cellar. When she reached the bedchamber, she hollered for help. She called for anyone she could — yeomen, guards, staff, even Walsingham in case he was nearby.

When the sounds of running footsteps neared, she ran back down into the cellar, her gaze flitting between Iomhar and the barrels. She had to make the place safe, or there was still the chance of an explosion. She lifted the lid off the barrel Iomhar had opened, finding it was full, then lifted the next. She grew still when she found the barrel empty. There was nothing inside it, not even a grain of gunpowder.

She opened the next three barrels, finding them just as empty as the other one. Covering her mouth with her hands, she dropped to her knees beside the unconscious Iomhar.

"It is not enough," she muttered to herself. It was enough for an explosion, but not one large enough to destroy the place, and certainly not enough to reach the queen's rooms. These barrels were a decoy.

"Iomhar?" She bent down toward him as yeomen began to appear in the cellar. Still, he didn't respond.

"That is a barrel of gunpowder. Get it somewhere safe and make sure there are no sparks." She issued the order quickly, never rising from where she was. Reaching toward Iomhar's mouth, she felt in front of his lips, searching for his breath. It came strongly, showing he was still very much there, even if he was not responding to her.

Once the yeomen had taken the barrel out, she pulled at Iomhar's arms, trying to draw him to his feet.

"Iomhar, you need to wake up," she begged. He barely moved until she slapped his cheek. It stirred him instantly, his eyes shooting open before another grunt of pain escaped him.

"Did ye slap me?" he asked wearily.

"Tell me another way to wake you up and I will do it. You have to stand." She snatched Lord Ruskin's pistol from the floor and pushed it into her belt before pulling on Iomhar's arms. He didn't argue with her. She drew him to his feet, but he tilted and nearly fell again. Kit ran round and caught him, forcing him upward. "Lean on me," she whispered, drawing him toward the door.

"Kit, be honest with me," he said as she pushed him onto the stairs. "Am I dying?"

"No."

"Ye are still a bad liar."

# CHAPTER 16

"Search for an intruder," Kit ordered one of the gentleman-at-arms, who helped her to haul Iomhar up the steps and into the guest chamber. "He was wearing a yeoman's robes and has pale blue eyes and fair hair."

"Yes, ma'am," the man nodded and hurried off.

Kit pushed Iomhar to stand and drew him to the door, but he didn't move. "Iomhar, you could die if you do not start moving. I need to get you to the physician."

"At this moment, walking seems like the greatest task in this world," Iomhar said quietly.

"Move, or I will do this." She stood on his foot, making him wince.

"I am in enough pain as it is," he groaned, but he stumbled forward, sometimes leaning more on Kit and at other times pressing against the wall.

As they stepped through the first doorway, they nearly fell, prompting Kit to wrap her arm around Iomhar's waist. She had to be careful to avoid his wound, but her movements still pulled on his belt.

"In the name of the wee man!" he bellowed as they hastened forward.

"That's it. Keep cursing, as long as it keeps you awake."

"Did I sleep?" Iomhar asked, his brows knitting together.

"Blood loss." Kit drew him forward into the courtyard, trying to take the shortest path. She knew the physicians and the apothecary rested in a chamber off the same corridor as the queen's rooms, so that they were nearby if needed. She had to get him that far if he had a chance of surviving.

"Of all the ways I pictured seeing that man again, I didn't think it would be like that. I vowed to demand the truth from him, to know who killed my father," Iomhar murmured. *"Tha mi duilich, Athair."*

"Iomhar? What was that?" Kit shoved him toward a closed door at the other end of the corridor.

"Gaelic," he whispered. "For my ears only."

She frowned, longing to know what he had muttered to himself as they continued through the corridors.

"Thank ye."

"Thank me? What on earth are you thanking me for?" she said in outrage, trying to concentrate on hauling him forward. "Do me a favour and stop wasting your energy on speaking. Use it to walk instead; I do not have the strength to put you over my shoulder."

"I'd like to see ye try," he muttered with a laugh before he broke off, wincing. "Thank ye for this. For trying."

"Do not thank me yet," she said firmly.

Silence fell between them as she pulled him up the stairs. This was the hardest part of their journey, with one of Iomhar's arms slung over her shoulders and his other one reaching for the banister to pull himself upward, yet his feet appeared reluctant to follow. As they stumbled onto the landing, Kit had to wrap both arms around his torso to stop him from tumbling back down the steps.

"Aye, ye are certainly grasping on to me now."

"How else am I supposed to get you to a physician?"

"And here I thought ye wanted to do it."

"How can you jest?" she cried out impatiently, hurrying him further forward. They were getting closer to the physician's room. Angling Iomhar to face the closed door, she kicked it open. It swung wide, revealing that just one of the physicians was inside, bent over a pewter trencher with a spoon halfway to his lips. "He needs help. A rapier wound."

"Lay him down. Here." The physician gestured toward the table in front of him where he had been eating his dinner, thrusting the trencher aside along with his tankard. Kit shoved Iomhar toward it, aware that with his body growing weaker, she was in danger of dropping him at any second. "Havers! Morgan! I need you!" the physician roared.

Kit pulled Iomhar further up the table as he lay back, his head thudding against the surface.

Another physician and the apothecary appeared, both standing in the doorway for a second like children called to a hanging.

"Do not stand there!" Kit yelled. "Do something!"

They moved toward the first physician to discuss what to do.

"Kit?" Iomhar's head turned to her as she was ushered down the table, away from Iomhar's wound and toward his face. The skin above his beard was pure white, almost as white as the two scars across his cheek. His breathing was laboured too.

"Keep breathing," she whispered, leaning down toward him.

When Havers went to pull back the belt and reveal the wound, Iomhar's eyes scrunched closed, and he yelped through gritted teeth.

"He needs something for the pain," Kit begged, looking to the apothecary beside her.

Morgan shook his head. "The pain can be borne. The priority is saving his life." As he spoke, he tossed a bandage to her. When she looked at him questioningly, he gestured to the wound on her hand, urging her to wrap it around her wrist where Lord Ruskin had cut her.

The words unsettled her, drawing her gaze back to Iomhar. His eyes had opened once more, a smirk quivering on his lips.

"Told ye I was dying."

"You think now is the time for a jest?" she asked angrily.

"I wish to die laughing, not afraid, Kit."

"You are not going to die!" She was insistent, yet the roar of pain that came from him as Havers pulled back his shirt and doublet drowned her words. She thrust her hands into her hair, pulling at the locks in fear.

"Kit, I need ye to listen to me," Iomhar said, his voice quiet.

"Stop breathing so fast," she begged him, resting her elbows on the table so that she was at his level.

"Remind me to tell ye the same when ye are lying here."

"I very nearly was," Kit muttered, remembering how Iomhar had stood in the way of Lord Ruskin's rapier. "What did you have to do that for?" she asked wildly, tapping him on the shoulder in reprimand. "Iomhar, you could have killed yourself."

He turned his gaze from her, adjusting his head so that he was staring up at the ceiling. Havers, Morgan and the other physician were all bent over the wound, working fast and calling to one another about what they needed to do to close it up. "I wasn't going to watch ye die, Kit." He refused to look at her as he spoke. "I could not do it."

Kit felt her mouth go dry. She dropped to the floor, clinging to the side of the table. Iomhar turned to look at her. "Stop speaking as if this is the last that we shall talk to each other," she pleaded. He smiled sadly, but it did not last long. "I will not watch you die, Iomhar."

"Then ye know what I felt." He nodded to her. "I do not regret it, Kit."

She felt tears filling her eyes but covered them quickly.

"Kit, I need ye to do something."

"Of course. What is it?" she murmured, lowering her hands. One tear leaked out of her eye, running slowly down her cheek.

"If I die, ye'll have to write to my brother and my mother. The address ye'll find at my home, in the study."

"Iomhar, stop this. You are not going to die. Is he?" She turned to the apothecary beside her. Morgan refused to meet her gaze, peering at the wound instead.

"Kit…" Iomhar whispered. His hand had lifted, and he placed his palm to her cheek. The touch at any other time would have startled her enough to make her rear back, but this time, she didn't move. He used his thumb to wipe away the tear. "Do not cry."

His eyes fluttered and she gasped.

"He's fading," Kit called to the physicians beside her. Havers reached for his other wrist, checking his pulse as Iomhar's hand dropped from Kit's cheek.

"He's alive. He's passing out."

"It's the blood loss," Morgan confirmed, as Iomhar's eyes closed completely.

Kit said nothing. She stared at the still form of Iomhar, unable to move or utter another word. He was breathing, that was plain to see from his parted lips and the way his chest moved up and down, but she had no idea how much longer he could hold on. The white linen strips around his wound were bright red.

"Kit?" a voice called from the doorway.

She lifted her eyes from Iomhar to peer over the heads of the physicians. Walsingham stood in the open doorway, watching her with a grave expression. He beckoned for her to come away.

Slowly, Kit stood, finding it hard to walk away from Iomhar's side. The blank expression on his face showed he was not aware of her being there anymore. He was somewhere else entirely. She walked to the door, where Walsingham hurried her outside.

"What happened?" he asked, his voice quiet and strained. "The yeomen are searching. Who are they looking for?"

"Lord Ruskin. He is dressed as a yeoman," Kit said, sniffing and trying to wipe away another tear. "There is a cellar blocked up beneath the guest chambers. He had placed gunpowder there."

Walsingham slowly turned away, leaning on a wall nearby. "He is the one responsible for this?"

"I believe so." Kit nodded. "He was the one who wrote to Lady Gifford too."

"Did he help her to escape the Tower?"

"The conversation did not continue long enough for me to find out." Kit's words left a brief silence between them, broken only by the murmurs inside the room. "How did he know of that chamber, though? We did not know of it."

"Enough whispers for me to hear of it," Walsingham said. "He must have heard of it from a friend within these walls. What of the gunpowder?"

"I think it was a decoy," Kit said, leaning on the closed door as she turned to face Walsingham. "It was not enough to blow up the palace."

"I do not suppose there is any chance of Lord Ruskin getting such a thing wrong? That it could be a genuine mistake?"

"No." Kit shook her head. "Iomhar described him as a military man. He would know how much gunpowder was needed."

Walsingham nodded slowly. "Lord Ruskin did this?" he asked, gesturing to the door.

"Yes. He was aiming for me," Kit whispered, finding it difficult to utter the words.

Walsingham cursed under his breath and pushed off the wall. "I cannot fault Iomhar's devotion to you, Kit."

The words only brought more pain. Another tear escaped and she hastily brushed it away.

"These tears worry me."

Kit sniffed and stood up straight. "I am as weak as the next person," she said in surprise. "How do you wish me to react to this? As if it has not happened? Or as if it does not matter?"

"Iomhar's devotion to you I can handle," Walsingham said with sudden harshness. "But yours ... it displeases me."

Kit stood taller, tipping her chin upwards. "I never said I was devoted. He is my friend. I do not want to see him die."

"You are too dependent on him. Stop the tears, Kit, and find your courage. If Lord Ruskin is loose in this palace, then no good comes from you standing here in this corridor, crying."

Kit felt the insult strongly and turned away, unable to look at Walsingham again. Her feet took her from the room, but her mind did not go with her. Her thoughts stayed with Iomhar and the physicians who were trying to stave off his death.

# CHAPTER 17

Kit lifted the net curtain and peered into the queen's bedchamber, finding her surrounded by her closest ladies-in-waiting. Lady Hunsdon sat by her side on the bed, pouring out a small glass of mead in the hope of tempting her appetite. Lady Stafford was on the queen's other side, holding her hand. Lady Hardwick was at the very end of the bed, her face pinched with an anxiety that Kit had not seen before.

The queen turned to the door, her dark eyes fixing on Kit with surprising intensity. She lifted her free hand to Lady Hunsdon and pressed it over the glass of mead to get her attention.

"What is it, Your Majesty?" Lady Hunsdon asked, leaning toward her. The queen nodded in Kit's direction. "I will send her away."

"No, you misunderstand, Anne," the queen murmured, her voice a little stronger than the last time Kit had heard it. She beckoned Kit forward. "A minute alone. That is what I need."

Lady Hunsdon appeared far from pleased, but she did as the queen asked, beckoning the others out of the room with a flick of her fingers. As Kit stepped in, Lady Hunsdon inched past her with a lingering look that she couldn't quite decipher. Once the room was empty, Kit approached the queen.

She was far from the image of grandeur and majesty that Kit had first seen in Hampton Court, but neither was she the wizened woman she'd been the day before.

"Are you surprised, Miss Scarlett?" the queen asked, with her head propped up on cushions and her red hair streaking across. "I am recovering, am I not?"

Kit moved forward to the side of the bed where Lady Stafford had been sitting. She took the chair, perching on the very edge. "I am pleased to see the change, Your Majesty," she said heartily.

"I heard from Anne that you are the one I have to thank for not meeting death yesterday," the queen said, her dark eyes flicking over Kit with such alacrity that she shifted in her seat. "I was not ready to greet God, nor to see my father again. I expect him to be waiting there for me, once I am gone from this world."

Kit turned her head to the side, intrigued to hear the queen speak of such things.

"I have surprised you, I can see it. Well, let me surprise you again." The queen lifted a hand and pointed at the mead glass. "First, pass me that mead, Miss Scarlett." Kit turned to the table where the glass had been placed and lifted it toward the queen. She took it with shaky fingers, before pressing it to her lips and sipping delicately. "Second, I wish you to do me a great favour. Go into that coffer you see on the far side of the room. That one there, beneath the curtains."

Kit turned to see where the queen was nodding and hurried to the coffer.

"You will find a small compartment in the lid, one that should not be there. Bring me what you find inside it."

A small block of wood had been nailed to the lid, allowing for a slim space in which something could be hidden. Delving her hand inside, Kit pulled out something that was cold and hard. Lifting it free of its hiding place, she discovered it was a gold ring encrusted with rubies. The stone across its peak was surrounded by much smaller and finer stones.

Holding the ring out in front of her, Kit returned to the queen and passed it to her. The queen took it with surprising eagerness, even finding the strength to lift herself off the pillows. She clasped the ring to her chest for a second, sighing, before slipping the band over her finger.

"You do not ask me what it is," she said with a small smile.

"It is not my place to ask," Kit murmured, feeling out of place. She glanced back to the doorway of the chamber, wondering if the ladies were watching them together, but there was no one there.

"In here is a person I am not permitted to speak of." The queen reached down to the ring and lifted the top stones. It peeled back like a lid, revealing two miniature portraits, no bigger than the pad of Kit's thumb. Kit leaned forward, her eyes flitting over the portraits in surprise. One was of the queen herself, that was plain to see, but the other was not so easy to discern. "I thought I would see her too last night, waiting for me after I died. I often wonder what she will say to me."

Kit didn't answer. She rather felt that the queen just wished to air thoughts she felt uncomfortable discussing with her ladies.

"You still do not ask me who it is." The queen smiled a little more. "Would you care to venture a guess?"

"Someone you cannot speak of, so…" Kit hung her head a little, realising who could be in the picture. There was one name that appeared to be banished from Hampton Court, even to this day. The woman once labelled 'the whore queen'. "Your mother, Your Majesty."

The queen neither confirmed nor denied it. She simply smiled a little more and closed the ring up, before holding her hand to her heart with the ring upon it. The simple touch was a meaningful one, making Kit's eyes sting for a moment with the threat of tears.

"Thank you, Miss Scarlett," the queen whispered, her eyes closed. "As much as I wish to see her, I was not ready to die."

"I will protect you, Your Majesty. In any way I can." Kit spoke the words firmly.

It was what she had been raised for, what she had been trained for, yet there was more to it. Seeing the queen as vulnerable as this brought the fear of the moment into focus. Above everything else, a woman's life had been threatened and she was scared. Kit longed to take away that fear.

"I hear from Lady Hunsdon that there is now another in this place who is fighting death." The queen opened her eyes, turning her narrow chin in Kit's direction. "A friend of yours."

Kit leaned on the edge of the bed and turned her eyes down, away from the queen. Her thoughts were filled with Iomhar, but she was not sure she could bring herself to talk of him at that moment.

"How does he fare, Miss Scarlett?"

"The physicians would not tell me anything," Kit whispered. "We must wait longer yet to know."

"That is what they kept telling me. Physicians! I am beginning to think they know nothing really." The queen laughed, sounding hollow and weak. "They bleed me to bleed out the poison, yet I only feel weaker after."

When the queen gestured for the glass of mead again, Kit proffered it, startled to find the queen looking at her.

"As I lay here yesterday, thinking I was to die, do you know what I thought of, Miss Scarlett?"

"What, Your Majesty?"

"I thought of all the things I wanted to say to those I loved, that I had not the strength to say." She flicked her gaze toward the doorway, evidently thinking of her ladies-in-waiting. "I am being careful to say all that I wish to now, so that when that time comes, I will have no regrets." Turning her focus back to Kit, she flattened her lips together, pausing. "You have saved my life on more than one occasion now, Miss Scarlett, and I am not sure I have thanked you properly for it. So, I thank you now."

"I require no thanks, Your Majesty."

"I will give it, nonetheless." She removed the ring from her finger and passed it back to Kit, lowering her voice to a whisper. "Hide it for me again. I do not want my ladies whispering about it. Then send Anne to me. I need her company."

"Yes, Your Majesty." Kit stood, sensing her dismissal. She returned the ring to its hiding place before leaving the room, finding Lady Hunsdon in the withdrawing chamber. "Lady Hunsdon, Her Majesty asks for you."

Lady Hunsdon nodded, rushing forward before stopping in front of Kit, her arm outstretched. "I wished to speak to you, Miss Scarlett," she murmured uncertainly. She looked behind her, as if wary of being overheard by the others, before turning back to Kit, her hands fidgeting. "Thank you, for what you did. You may be a strange sort of woman…" At the words, Kit bristled, standing taller and jerking her chin higher. "Yet I see you are a good woman too. You saved her, from someone I never even suspected capable of … well, of what she tried to do. You have kept our queen safe."

"Do not thank me yet, Lady Hunsdon." Kit's simple words stopped Lady Hunsdon's fidgeting. "This is not over yet."

"But you stopped Lady Gifford."

"She is not the only one who threatens the queen." Kit glanced over her shoulder to the chamber she had just left. The queen was improving, but she was not yet recovered, meaning that what Kit had to propose could be difficult yet. "We must move the queen."

"Move her? You must be able to see she is still in no fit state to go anywhere —"

"Then let it be soon." Kit's mind shot to the empty gunpowder barrels. It was still possible that the real gunpowder was hidden somewhere in the palace, with Lord Ruskin biding his time before he set it alight. "She must be moved. In disguise, if necessary, but she is not safe yet, Lady Hunsdon."

Kit walked away, not letting Lady Hunsdon delay her any further.

Kit hovered outside of the physicians' room, trying her best to gain access. Each time she knocked on the door she was refused entry, to the point where the apothecary came outside to speak to her.

"Not yet." Morgan spoke calmly, though Kit could not be so calm.

"All I want is to see him."

"Then you must wait longer, for there is more we must do. How are your wounds?" Morgan looked at the cut on her hand and pulled back her sleeve, checking the bindings, though Kit barely took notice.

"What? What is it you are doing to him?" Kit asked. "You must have already sewn up his wound."

"It must be undone again."

"What did you say?" Kit hissed as she stepped toward Morgan.

Morgan backed up, colliding with the door behind him. "There is something wrong internally. Either the wound was sewn up wrong, or there is internal bleeding."

"You do not know?" Kit's voice grew angrier.

"Leave him with us longer. He is still fighting this, for now."

"For now? You think that brings comfort?" Kit stepped toward him again, so furiously that the apothecary retreated completely this time.

"Go, Miss Scarlett. Leave this to us." He closed the door on her and locked it tight as she reached for the door handle. No matter how many times she turned that handle, it would not open. She debated kicking the door down.

"Kit?" Walsingham's voice brought her to a halt. Turning her head, she found him walking down the corridor toward her, his manner agitated. "This is not your post. You should either be by the queen's side or searching for the gunpowder."

"You have searched many times and not found it. Does that not rather suggest it is ingeniously hidden?" There was a wildness to her tone that appeared to take Walsingham by surprise. He stepped back and his black eyes widened.

"It does no good for you to stand outside his door like a pup."

"That is not what I am doing." She pushed against the door another time. "I merely wish to see how he fares."

"No doubt the apothecary has told you. Now, leave it be." Walsingham reached for her arm. His fingers latched over the wound that was still hidden beneath her doublet. She had to bite the inside of her mouth to stop herself from complaining. It would have been simple enough to push Walsingham off her, but she could never imagine being violent toward him.

He drew her far down the corridor to the top of the staircase, where he eventually released her. Kit turned and grabbed the banister, trying to hide the fact that he had gripped her wound and hurt her.

"Go to your post, Kit," he warned her once more.

As he moved down the stairs, his stride purposeful, Kit found words falling from her lips. She had a feeling it had something to do with what the queen had said to her, about regretting leaving things unsaid. The knowledge that Iomhar could die at any second made everything he had recently asked of her come into focus.

"Walsingham?" she called, making his pace slow on the stairs, though he did not stop. "There is something I need to ask of you."

She saw that image in her mind once again. She was beneath the water, struggling to the surface, with the shadow of a woman walking away, leaving her there. Then Walsingham was reaching down toward her, and his bony hand took hers.

"What is it?" Walsingham called back.

"How did we meet?" Kit murmured. Despite the quietness of the words, Walsingham froze, tripping on a step as he turned back to her with humour in his face.

"You know how we met. Have I not told you the story many times? You pulled —"

"On your cloak, begging in the streets," Kit said hurriedly. "I know, I have heard the tale, but is it the truth?"

Walsingham said nothing. He stared at her, his face impassive. Kit walked toward where he stood, halting two steps above him.

"I have a feeling we met another way. Is it true?" she asked, surprised to find herself nervous to describe the image at all.

"Where has this come from?" Walsingham asked dismissively. He turned away from her and hurried down the steps, putting distance between them. "This is not the time, Kit. Maybe all that has happened has upset you of late, but that is no reason —"

"You did not answer my question." Kit's words brought him to a stop at the bottom of the steps.

"This is madness," Walsingham muttered. "You know how we met, and you know why I brought you home — to save you from dying on the streets like the other poor beggar children. What has brought this up now?"

"I have no memory of begging." Kit shook her head. "Tell me this, then: if we met on the streets, why do I have this idea of being underwater, with you reaching down to pull me out?" She finally uttered the words, watching as Walsingham turned pale, even paler than normal.

"It is called a nightmare, Kit. You had it repeatedly when you were a child. That is all." He flicked his head away and walked forward. "This is the end of this discussion. Return to your post."

Within seconds he was gone, with his heeled boots clicking against the floorboards so loudly that they echoed around the corridor. Kit stared after him, her lips parted and a hand clutching the banister.

# CHAPTER 18

Kit leaned against the wall that led up to the gatehouse of Hampton Court. In the distance, the sun was beginning to fade, slipping past the palace in such a way that it made the red bricks appear redder, as if they were burning already.

"Do you have anything to report?" Walsingham's voice urged Kit to pull herself straight, looking down the other side of the wall to see him approach. She had not seen him since their conversation that morning, and now he stopped some distance away from her. She could sense he had no wish to open such a discussion again.

Bringing one foot up on the wall, she rested her chin against her knee, looking down at him.

"We did another search, but no, we found nothing," Kit said.

Walsingham seemed uncomfortable in her presence, something he had never been before. He barely looked at her, choosing instead to turn his eyes on the yeomen guards that passed them, performing their duties of locking the palace up for the night. "This is not helping," he muttered, gnashing his teeth. "So many searches and not a thing to show for it." He rubbed his hands over his face and turned his body away.

"We need to try another way." Kit glanced up at the palace behind her, thinking of what had happened there only two days before. "Lord Ruskin is behind this. From what Iomhar has said, that man cares too much for the finer things in life to live on the streets for a few days. When we were in Northumberland, I heard tales of Lord Ruskin spending his days in Alnwick Castle, with the Earl of Northumberland's son."

"I do not understand you, Kit."

"I mean he must be hiding somewhere." Kit pushed off from the wall and jumped down to Walsingham's side, tired of him refusing to look at her. Her action made him glance toward her, but it was not for very long. "If he is in London, then he will have found somewhere to stay. Maybe there is a way to track where he has gone. If we find him, then maybe that is the way to stop the gunpowder going off."

"Yes, yes, that is a good thought." Walsingham spoke distractedly. "Go home, Kit, get some sleep. Tomorrow, start your search for Lord Ruskin."

"Home?" Kit spluttered in surprise, following him as he strode back toward the palace. "You wished me to stay here; why the change?"

"It will do you good not to be in this palace all the time."

"You mean it will do me good to be unable to check on Iomhar," Kit muttered bitterly. As they reached the gatehouse where two yeoman guards stood, Walsingham clicked his fingers at them. They both stepped forward, thrusting their pikes together to block Kit's path. She stumbled to a stop. "Are you threatening me, Walsingham?"

He faced her from where he stood on the other side of the pikes. "No," he said slowly, "but I am stopping you from coming back into this palace. Go home. You are usually good at following orders."

Walsingham strode into the palace, leaving Kit staring between the yeomen with their pikes. She could have easily moved past them if she'd wished to, for they would be sluggish with their long and unwieldy weapons and she would be quick with her daggers, but she did not see the point in fighting. Sleep did not seem such an awful idea.

Standing outside of Iomhar's house, Kit lingered in the doorway, uncertain where else to go. She could have gone to her lodgings, but the memory of the shadow that had lurked by her door and the fact that someone had searched her rooms prevented her. It did not seem a safe place to go.

Knocking on the door, she waited for an answer, growing more and more impatient. Rain was beginning to fall, creating puddles around Kit's feet and running off the timber beams of the building. The door was opened at last by Elspeth, the elderly cook and housekeeper.

"My goodness!" Elspeth cried with a hand to her heart. "Miss Scarlett? You gave me a fright."

"My apologies," Kit said, trying to shake some of the water from her body as Elspeth stepped back, allowing her inside.

"Where is my master, Miss Scarlett? He hasn't been home for days."

Realising the news hadn't yet reached poor Elspeth's ears, Kit removed her hat fast out of respect and wrung the water out through the open door before turning to her.

"I have grave news," she said slowly. "He has been injured."

"How badly?" Elspeth tried to maintain a calm manner, but her bottom lip twitched. Kit struggled for words. Her silence seemed to speak volumes for Elspeth nodded, trembling as she stepped away. "Will he live?"

"We must wait to know," Kit murmured.

"Aye, very well." Elspeth gripped her skirts and reached for a handkerchief that she had pushed up her sleeve. "You have come to tell me, Miss Scarlett?"

"Yes, and to ask a favour," Kit said, glancing back to the windows that flanked the doors as the rain grew heavier. Each drop thrashed against the glass like a bullet, quickly turning into hail. "May I spend the night here? I would not wish to trouble you to make up a bed."

"Nonsense, Miss Scarlett. Aye, the master said you should always be welcome."

"He did?" Kit felt her eyebrows lift as she followed the beckoning hand of Elspeth.

"Oh, aye," Elspeth exclaimed, hurrying down the corridor. Kit had only taken a few steps when the portrait she had seen so often in Iomhar's home appeared beside her in the light that emanated from Elspeth's candle. That orange glow briefly flitted across the different faces of the children and the parents, lingering for a few seconds longer on Iomhar's face to Kit's mind, rather than any of the other figures.

"When did he say that?" Kit asked, hastening after Elspeth as the light faded from the portrait.

"Not that long ago," Elspeth said with a shrug. "I do not think he liked the idea of you in those lodgings, Miss Scarlett. He was always saying the door was easy to get by."

"Yes, he was right about that," Kit said.

"I'll have a room ready for you in no time. You take to the drawing room, Miss Scarlett. I'll fetch you something to warm your bones too; we need food on a night like this one."

Kit nodded, though she was uncertain whether she could bear the thought of food at all.

Once in the drawing room, she began to shed the wet clothes, tossing off the sodden doublet and hanging it from the mantelpiece over the fire to dry, and kicking off her boots to sit by the grate. She placed the weapons belt over a table beside the fire, being careful to keep Lord Ruskin's pistol away from the flames. Rather than taking any of the chairs, she sat on the rug, letting the heat of the fire dry her hair.

By the time she had lit candles and placed them along the fireplace to keep her company, Elspeth reappeared with a bowl of stew. The scent that wafted toward Kit was earthy and meaty, making her stomach growl.

"Get that down you, Miss Scarlett. Chuck stew. One of the master's favourites."

Kit thanked her and took the bowl in her hand, eating hurriedly, though after Elspeth left, she found it difficult to swallow at all. Her eyes kept flitting to the empty chair by the fireplace where she had seen Iomhar sit so often this last year. It remained firmly empty, no matter how much she stared at it.

After she had finished her meal, Elspeth returned, proffering ale for Kit to quench her thirst.

"Something arrived for the master today. I placed it on his writing bureau." Elspeth pointed to a small oak desk in the corner of the room, pushed under a window where the hail still thrashed beyond. "I do not suppose he will have a chance to open it now."

"Do you recognise the hand?" Kit asked, walking toward the desk.

"Aye, Miss Scarlett. It is from one of the master's brothers."

"Thank you, Elspeth. I will take it to him tomorrow." Kit waited until Elspeth had left the room once more before turning to the letter, breaking the seal and opening it up. She could remember where she had seen the handwriting before — it belonged to Niall, Iomhar's younger brother whom she had met in Northumberland.

She moved to the fireplace and held it toward the candles along the hearth, the better to see the black ink in the flames.

*Dear brother,*

*I have heard nothing. Aye, I wish I could say more than anything else in this world that I have heard of where Lord Ruskin has gone, but there is nay news.*

*Our brother grows restless every week. I know well enough being the Earl of Ross must be challenging for him. He faces the king's court daily with the constant need to improve his standing, but he cannot put his heart into it. He told me last week he asked the king once more if he had ever heard about what happened to our father, but the king silenced him quite readily, telling him it was high time we all gave up the hunt for our father's killer. It seems the king doesn't know what it is like to have a father's death haunting him.*

*Tell me more of what ye have found in Hampton Court. Do ye still believe the gunpowder to be related to Lord Ruskin's aims?*

*Now, there is another matter which I must speak to ye of. Our mother is restless. She longs to hear news of ye every day and longs to see ye even more. Come home, Iomhar. Even if it is for a short while. Aye, bring your lass with ye, the one who dresses in hose and a jerkin. I rather think she could bring a smile to our mother's face. We need all the excuses we can have for smiles these days.*

*Our mother grew serious the other day. She yearns to know who took her husband from her, but it seems her fear for us is now greater. She doesn't want our lives dominated by our hunt. My words seemed to fall on deaf ears. I cannot let it go, nay more than ye can, nor our brother can. She has accepted it, but I found her weeping in the early hours of the morning.*

*She cannot bear our lives to be like this forever, Iomhar. The sooner we find out the truth from Lord Ruskin, the better for all of us.*

*Write back to me soon.*

*Your brother,*

*Niall.*

Kit lowered the letter to the rug, being careful to keep it away from the flames and the damp spots. She had already known how devoted Iomhar was to finding out what had happened to his father, but the fact that it was a hunt that dominated the entire family was news to her. If Niall's letter was completely honest, then the whole family's happiness seemed to depend on the truth being learned from Lord Ruskin someday.

Standing with sudden purpose, Kit hurried to the writing bureau, taking ink and parchment. Using the address Niall had provided, she wrote to him. She was careful in the way she delivered the news of Iomhar's injury: *It was at Lord Ruskin's hand, but it was meant for me. Iomhar stepped forward and took the wound himself…*

Merely writing the words made tears spring to Kit's eyes. She didn't bother trying to fight them in the loneliness of the room. She let them slide down her cheeks, only wiping them away when they reached the bottom of her chin to stop them falling onto the letter.

She signed it off, promising to deliver news of Iomhar's health as soon as she could. She then sealed it with plain red wax that she melted in a candle flame, before pushing the letter away.

Once her task was done, she returned to Niall's letter, lifting it up and lingering over the words. Reading of Niall's suffering, his brother's, and his mother's brought into focus why Iomhar hunted Lord Ruskin. It was not just about discovering who had taken his father's life; it was about bringing the entire family peace.

Folding the letter up and returning it to the desk, she crossed the room. She hurried to the place where she had discarded her doublet and her weapons belt, taking the weapons one at a time and moving them to the table. She pushed away her daggers first, then reached for the pistol that she had snatched from the floor, the one that Lord Ruskin had left behind.

Lifting it high, she examined the markings across the hilt and along the barrel. If she was to track Lord Ruskin down, not just for the queen's sake, but for Iomhar's too, then this was the one clue she had. He must have secured the weapon from somewhere. It was possible he had brought it with him from Scotland, but it was also possible he had found it in London.

Kit turned the pistol over again in her hands, judging it to be one of the latest models of wheellocks, rather like the one Iomhar had been given. It was most likely to have been made in a city, either in London, Bristol or Edinburgh. Resting the pistol in the palm of her hand, she found there was something etched along the barrel.

Moving closer to the fire, she returned to her knees, the better to see in the firelight what was etched into the rosewood. There appeared to be a maker's initials, but they had been almost carved out, as if someone had taken a blade and scored against them. Kit smiled, recognising the action, for she had heard it talked about in Walsingham's conversations with other intelligencers: *The mark of a smuggled weapon. They try to hide who made the pistol.*

"A smuggled weapon," she said aloud, turning to the empty chair where Iomhar should have sat. She kept her eyes on it for a minute, speaking as if he was there. "It is a way to start, is it not? The smugglers…" She could already imagine what Iomhar would say to her. He would issue caution, tell her to think it through and not act on impulse. "I will be careful," she whispered, as if he could hear her.

# CHAPTER 19

The scent of sugar was strong in the air, mixed with rose water and honey. Kit's nose angled toward it as she peered around the corner of a timber frame building, leaning on the wood and gazing at the place the scent was wafting from. The door to the confectioner's shop was open wide, with the ground crunching beneath customers' feet where the sugar had been dropped onto the floor. Beyond the glass windows, comfits were pressed forward on little pewter trays. Some were dappled with sugar, others wrapped in pastry. Kit's eyes danced across the marchpane before she returned her focus to the door.

The confectioner was a buxom woman, with her curves pincered together around her waist by the string that held up her white apron. Her hair was tucked beneath a white muslin cloth and her thin nose was turned down toward all of her customers, thanks to her superior height. She had a smile for everyone that passed and was always waving.

Kit had to wait until the shop was quiet. The last customer left holding a handful of sweets that he had tucked away in a cloth. She hurried forward, crossing the street quickly and following the confectioner into the shop, where Kit closed the door harshly behind her.

The confectioner jumped, turning round with her hands pressed to her wide stomach and laughing. "Oh, dearie me, you gave me quite a start there, love. You must be eager for your comfits today. We do not often close the door here, not good for customers, see? Open it again will you, love?"

"I think we will keep it closed for now." Kit kept her foot firmly against the door and tilted her hat upward, showing she had no intention of opening it.

The confectioner turned round, her hands hovering over a table covered in sugar mice with string tails. Her eyes were wide with humour as she found Kit's face.

"Do you know, dearie, I really thought you were a boy then. My mistake, must be my eyes these days — growing tired, they are, from all the sugar in the air." She wafted a handkerchief.

Kit had had enough of the merry tone. She was in no mood to smile, especially when she knew the truth of the confectioner before her.

"I am not here for sweets." Kit spoke firmly. "I heard you have another trade you like to peddle, though where you keep your weapons hidden, I do not know. I see no marchpane large enough for a pistol to be hidden beneath." Her words brought the confectioner up short. The lady leaned on the table between them, pressing her weight downwards and staring at Kit, who kicked a bucket in front of the door to stop any more customers coming in. Slowly, she rounded the shop, checking each table in turn, but there was no sign of any weapons, only sugar work and comfits.

"I don't know what you're talking of, dearie," the lady said, her smile returning. It appeared quickly, as if it had been flicked into place. "Now, what can I do for you? Sugar mice? Or sugared lemons? Always a favourite."

Kit took hold of a marchpane block and pushed it across the table, smiling a little. "No harm in taking some marchpane as well, I suppose," she said.

"As well as what?" the confectioner asked, wrapping the marchpane up with a cloth and string.

"Where are your weapons?" Kit's question made the woman pause with the string before knotting it tightly. "I am not here to close your business. As far as I'm concerned, it must make you good money."

"Sugar is pricey, dearie, it pays me well. I need no other business."

Kit grew tired. She was hardly going to dally with this woman when the gunpowder hidden in Hampton Court could be lit at any moment. She took hold of a stand beside her, full of jellylike sugared fruits, and prodded it over, so that the sweets cascaded across the floor.

"Well, I am pleased to see that took your smile away," Kit said as the woman flinched at the crashing sound. "Would you like to continue this game, or shall I destroy something else? As you say, sugar is expensive, is it not? I suppose if I destroyed your entire shop, it would cost you a pretty penny to replace it." Kit lifted a pewter plate, across which were tiny, beaded confits with hard shells.

The plate was snatched from her grasp by the woman, who held it close to her bosom.

"You could have just asked kindly if you wanted a weapon."

"I tried that," Kit pointed out. "Where are they?"

The confectioner flicked her eyes to the other side of the room, nodding her head in the direction of another table. Cakes and icing populated this table, but the cloth beneath them was bobbly. Kit hastened to the table, lifting the cakes and pushing them to the side, along with the cloth. She found it was no table at all, but an open coffer, filled to the brim with weapons.

There were daggers, some cheap with blunted blades and others ornate with beautifully carved wooden handles. There was a crossbow discarded at one side of the box with all its bolts in place, but the most common items in the coffer were pistols. Each one was different, the wheellocks marred with use and scorched black. Some were ornate with engravings on the hilt, others utilitarian and plain. Kit reached for the nearest pistol, recognising the rosewood as being similar to the one in her belt. She lifted it high, analysing the barrel.

"How did you hear about me?" the confectioner asked from the other side of the shop. "I do not often get strangers in here asking for weapons."

"Let's say an acquaintance of mine has a weapon from you." Kit recognised the etching on the barrel. It was the same one as on Lord Ruskin's pistol, marred in the same manner and scratched out. "There may be a few black-market trades in London for weapons, but you are the only one near Hampton Court."

"Are you from the palace?" the woman asked excitedly, leaning forward on her table.

Kit chose not to answer and picked the pistol out from her belt, comparing the two. They were almost identical in build and decoration, along with the spoilt maker's mark.

"It's pricey, if you want it, dearie. Much more so than marchpane."

"I am not here to buy." Kit moved back to her and placed her pistol down on the table. "See this mark?" She gestured to it. "Just like this one, on my acquaintance's pistol. I want to know who you sold this one to."

The confectioner took the pistol off Kit, staring at her. "If I refuse to answer your questions?"

"Shall I push over something else?" Kit offered, tapping her boot against a nearby table. Clearly the confectioner didn't want to stand the risk. Making comfits was too expensive to waste everything that was in the shop. It could put her out of business.

She turned her eyes down to the weapon. "I recognise it," she said quietly. "It has an extra mark, here." She turned it over, pointing to a scratch Kit had not noticed on the hilt. "I was asked to save it for a special customer. I was given instructions by my supplier. They wanted this weapon to go to a particular man."

"Who?" Kit demanded, deepening her voice as she leaned on the table between them.

"Didn't give his name, dearie." She shook her head, placing the pistol back down.

"Did he say anything?"

"Little. Not from round here, though."

"Scottish?" Kit asked excitedly.

"Could be. Not good with accents me, but he was certainly not from here." The confectioner watched as Kit returned the pistol to her belt.

"What did he look like?" Kit asked.

"Fair hair. Pale face. Rather hooked nose. He asked for directions."

"To where?"

"Vine Street."

Kit jerked, nearly dropping the pistol as she placed it in her belt. It was the name of the road where her lodgings were. She went still as she realised who could have been that shadow waiting for her outside of her room.

Lord Ruskin had tried to kill her before. He had even sent a man to do the job for him in Northumberland, but it had failed. The revenge he wanted to take for his wife's death was incomplete.

"I am a fool," Kit whispered to herself. She should have known who had followed her from Hampton Court that day and hovered outside of her lodgings. Either it was Lord Ruskin himself, or he had sent another man to do the job again.

"You all right, dearie?" the confectioner asked, eyeing Kit closely.

"You said you were given instructions," Kit murmured, reaching for the marchpane. "You were told to keep the pistol here for this man. Who told you to do it?" As she threatened to pick up another pewter tray of comfits to destroy, the confectioner quickly took it away.

"Knepp. He gives me some weapons from time to time, and he asked me to keep this one to the side. Said the man that would come to collect it would know his name."

"Wait, Knepp? Is that what you said?" Kit's hand tightened around the marchpane.

"Yes."

"First name?"

"John Knepp," the confectioner said, her gaze flicking to the door as a customer tried to come in. The door jammed against the bucket. "One minute, dearie!" she called, her cheery tone back. She grabbed the discarded pistol and threw it into the coffer before covering it back over with the cloth and cakes.

Kit didn't move for a minute; she was too busy feeling something darken within her at this news. "Elderly, hunched, dark eyebrows and white hair?" she asked impatiently as the confectioner crossed behind her.

"You know him?" the confectioner asked, her foot hovering by the bucket, ready to kick it out of the way. Kit nodded, for she knew exactly who he was. "Then are we done?"

"Yes."

The confectioner kicked the bucket out of the way and warmly invited her customers into the shop. As they began to peruse, she turned back to Kit and held out her palm. "For the marchpane."

Kit dropped a coin into the woman's palm and rushed out of the door. If she was to find Knepp quickly, speak to him and get back to Hampton Court, she needed a horse.

Kit pulled the horse to a stop on the drive of Barn Elms, looking up at Walsingham's house with anger. Many times on the journey had she tried to persuade herself that there could be an honest explanation for why Walsingham's own gun man would be the one working with the confectioner and giving her a weapon to bestow on Lord Ruskin, yet she was struggling to think of anything that made sense.

If Walsingham had known what his gun man was up to, then it put everything she thought she knew about Walsingham into the shadows.

Rounding the house quickly, Kit pulled up by the servants' stairs. She had no wish to go inside, especially if Lady Sidney was there. It would be wasting time. Tossing the reins into the hands of a stable boy that ran forward, she hurried to the back door, knocking quickly. When the elderly steward, Mr Withers, answered, his eyebrows rose and his jowls shook.

"Miss Scarlett, you are not supposed to be here today. The master is not even here."

"That is fine, Withers. I am not here to see him." She pushed past him. His outrage was apparent as he threw insults after her. She ignored them all, rushing to the cellar door. Once she disappeared down the staircase, the insults faded. She reckoned Withers was relieved that she had not gone into the main part of the house.

As she hurried into the belly of the cellar, her boots on the stone floor must have alerted Knepp to her presence, for he came running across the room.

"Shoes off, weapons off, no sparks down here, remember?" he said loudly. Kit kicked off her shoes and took off her weapons belt, casting them onto a table laid out for just such a purpose, though she lifted one of her daggers and thrust it toward Knepp.

The threat was clear as Knepp stumbled to a halt in his soft-padding slippers, looking up at her with the skin around his eyes tightening.

"I wanted to make sure I had your attention," she said softly. Knepp stumbled back further. She advanced forward, not letting him get far. "Knepp, explain to me why you are giving the confectioner in Wolsey Road a pistol for a man called Lord Ruskin to collect?"

"I-I didn't know that was his name." Knepp stepped back and panicked, thrusting up his hands and pointing to the weapons behind him. "You cannot bring that in here! What if there is a spark? All this gunpowder!"

"Have you left anything else for this man to pick up? Gunpowder?"

"No." Knepp shook his head. "I was given the one instruction, to provide a pistol, that was all."

"Does Walsingham know about this?" Kit demanded. Seeing she had Knepp's full attention, she tossed the dagger onto the table and advanced toward him. Grabbing his collar, she towed him across the room, heading in the direction of the weapons.

"No, of course not." Knepp spoke quickly, but Kit couldn't be certain he was not lying. Something Iomhar had once said was burning in her mind: *How can ye ever be certain if a spymaster can be trusted, Kit?*

"Show me the pistols."

Knepp was marched forward, with Kit holding onto his collar. When he pointed to a rack of weapons, she released him at last, looking at the pistols. On one rack, she saw wheellock pistols like Iomhar's, and another was full of pistols that bore the same marks and patterns as the one they had taken from Lord Ruskin.

"How did this happen?" she asked impatiently. "Who gave you this instruction and why did you follow it?"

"They paid me." Knepp looked down miserably. "My daughter is unwell. She cannot work. The money ... it was too much to refuse."

Kit was tempted to believe him, but she couldn't be certain that Walsingham did not know of this. "You already peddle the pistols, do you not? For your own gain?" she asked, remembering what the confectioner said about Knepp giving her some weapons.

"Walsingham never notices they are gone," he said quietly. "It pays. I must help my daughter somehow."

Kit felt the fury pump through her. She reached toward Knepp once more and grabbed him by his jerkin, raising him so that he had to stand on the balls of his feet. "You gave a weapon to a man who has planted gunpowder in Hampton Court. *That* is what you have done. This is not about money; it is about the death of our queen — do you understand what you have done now?" She seethed, watching as Knepp trembled in her grasp. He began to shake his head, clearly not wanting to believe it.

Kit released him and pushed him so far that he nearly collided with the weapons. She shot him one last glare before she walked back the way she had come, hurrying past woollen sheets that hung from the ceiling to the floor, protecting barrels of gunpowder.

"What will you do?" Knepp called, hobbling after her. "What happens now?"

"Walsingham must know of what you have done," Kit said with finality, putting her weapons belt back on. She just had to hope that when Walsingham said he knew nothing of this, she would believe him.

# CHAPTER 20

Kit waited for hours in her street, standing in the doorway opposite her lodgings to see if Lord Ruskin would appear, but he never did. It didn't seem to matter how many times Kit checked over her shoulder either, looking to see if she was being followed. There was never a shadow behind her and no sign that anyone had been tracking her.

Giving up on the prospect of being able to catch Lord Ruskin that evening, Kit made her way to Hampton Court, determined to see Walsingham. The yeoman guards thought twice about letting her past the gatehouse when she arrived on a cart, but when she declared she had a message for Walsingham, important for the queen's safety, they let her pass.

Traipsing through the corridors, she found Walsingham eventually. He was sitting in the great hall that had been built by King Henry, slumped in his chair and staring at the wooden ceiling, as if it could offer up some answers. There was no one else in the room. Alone, he was muttering something under his breath with his palms pressed together.

Kit inched forward into the room. Her boots on the floor alerted him to her presence and he turned his head downwards, but he didn't stop mumbling, not yet. As he unfurled his hands and lowered them to his knees, he lifted his chin toward Kit.

"Give me some good news, Kit, something," he begged, his voice weak.

"I take it your continued searches have found nothing," she said, startled by how firm her own voice was. She was too suspicious and resentful of the fact he was keeping secrets from her to be kind to him. His grey brows knitted together.

"No. What has your search yielded?"

"This." Kit took out the unloaded pistol from her belt and tossed it toward him as she stopped a few steps away in the middle of the great hall. Walsingham caught it, holding his hands up to shield himself from the blow.

"What is it?" he asked.

"The pistol we took from Lord Ruskin. Do you not recognise it? Curious, because it came from your own weapon store."

Walsingham became still. "Do not play games with me today, Kit. I am in no mood."

"What kind of a fool do you think I am to jest about this?" she scoffed at him, taking a step forward and pointing down at the weapon. "That was smuggled out of your store by Knepp and given to a confectioner on Wolsey Road, left there for Lord Ruskin to collect."

Walsingham stood and pushed the pistol back into Kit's hand. He seemingly could not bear to touch it anymore. "You are certain of this?"

"It is beyond doubt. What I do doubt is why Knepp gave it to this confectioner."

"Do not utter another word, Kit," Walsingham said, his already bleak gaze darkening further. "I will not have you of all people suspect me."

"Then prove me wrong." She thrust the pistol back into her weapons belt. "This is traced to your very door. You would suspect any other man who was in your position, would you not?" Her question silenced him. He blinked a few times, breathing deeply until he was practically wheezing.

"You doubt me?" he asked eventually, through gritted teeth. "Everything I have ever done is for the good of our queen, Kit, surely you see that."

"I thought it was, but then explain this to me." Kit's voice grew louder, more insistent.

"How can I when I knew nothing of it?" Walsingham asked, holding his hands out. "Knepp has a sick daughter. If I was to place a wager on it, I would say any man who knew this could use it against him, offering him money."

"They did," Kit agreed with a sharp nod. "That does not mean you did not know about it."

"Kit, have you taken leave of all good sense?" Walsingham raged. Kit was startled but stood her ground, refusing to back away. "Do you not know me by now?" Walsingham took a step toward her, placing a palm on his chest. "Have we not lived side by side for years, since you were a child?"

"I never said I was ungrateful," Kit muttered.

Walsingham barely let her finish, throwing his hands up in the air. "You have seen me raise you to protect our queen, teaching you all the skills you needed to do so. Why would I do that if I was against our queen, Kit? Answer me that!"

"You would not be the first man whose mind has been changed —"

"I have had enough of this." Walsingham turned away, flapping his arms in her direction. His loose black doublet billowed around his shoulders like the wings of a raven. "I do not have to explain myself to you. Not when you are talking such nonsense. It is your grief that has addled your mind, that is all. You are too busy worrying about Iomhar to think clearly."

"An interesting theory, but an incorrect one."

"Kit!" he snapped, whipping round to face her. "Go home. God's wounds, go home, and do not ask me such things as this again, or you will soon find yourself without a home, job or protector. Is that understood?" He pushed a finger toward her chest.

Kit flicked her gaze down at that hand. "Give me a reason to trust you and I will." Her calm voice broke through his anger, and he stared at her in wonder.

"Have I not given you reason enough already?"

"You are keeping a secret from me," she whispered, watching as Walsingham lifted his hands and steepled them over his mouth.

"You wish to return to our conversation about your nightmares? They were merely terrors you had when you were a child. You dreamt often of being underwater. I can only assume the dream has come back."

"Did I see someone leaving me there in those nightmares?" Kit asked quietly, folding her arms across her chest.

Walsingham seemed stunned. "Did you see their face?"

"Why ask me that?" Kit demanded. "Why ask me that if this is all merely the dream of an imaginative child?"

"Enough!" Walsingham roared. This silenced her, reminding her of a moment when she was young in Seething Lane. He had roared at her once when she had come in from the streets, her gown covered in mud after she had played with some of the other children who lived nearby. "It was a dream, Kit. Nothing more."

She said nothing. She had the answer she wanted to hear. But if there was no truth in it, why did it make him so angry? Why would he ask if she had seen the face of the person who had left her in the water?

"Go home," he ordered again. "Get some sleep. I will need you back tomorrow for another search. Yes?"

Kit said nothing for a minute, too busy observing the frantic way in which he moved back and forth.

"Yes, Kit?" he repeated impatiently.

"Yes," she muttered.

"Good," he barked and walked past her, hovering for a second to issue another order in her ear. "And do not let me hear you question where my loyalties lie again." His shoes struck the floorboards loudly as he left the room.

Kit hovered by the door of the queen's chambers, waiting for Lady Hunsdon to come to speak to her. She had no intention of following Walsingham's orders and going home. Defying him no longer felt so dangerous or wrong.

As Lady Hunsdon appeared at the door, she had a smile on her face.

"How does she fare?" Kit asked hurriedly.

"A little better. She cannot stand yet, but she is eating again. It could improve her strength." Lady Hunsdon seemed anxious, her voice more strained than usual. "You mentioned the possibility of moving the queen?"

"Yes, I think it a wise thing," Kit said, her eyes flicking into the privy chamber where the other ladies were gathered. "For everyone's safety."

"Where would she go?"

"One of the other palaces, but in disguise," Kit whispered, so only Lady Hunsdon could hear her. "Do you think it possible?"

"If she continues to recover at this rate, then yes, I do, but certainly not tonight. Maybe tomorrow or the next day. The subject must be broached with her. I do not think she will take kindly to being drawn from her sickbed." Lady Hunsdon's voice had a tremor to it. "Yet you believe it to be the safest thing?"

"I do. The danger has not passed, and we would be foolish to rejoice in the queen's recovery when the threat still hangs over our heads," Kit said quietly. "Is there any chance you could persuade her? When Walsingham and I broached the subject last, she was not keen on the idea, but she was worse then. As she is recovering, she might not be so against the idea."

"Yes, it is possible." Lady Hunsdon turned to the door. "Leave it with me, Miss Scarlett. Allow me to persuade the queen. If her mind can be changed, Dorothy and I are the ones to do it."

Kit smiled, grateful for Lady Hunsdon's help. To her surprise, Lady Hunsdon returned that smile before she disappeared back into the room.

Leaving the queen's chambers behind, Kit walked away, heading through the corridors and past the gentlemen-at-arms that were guarding this part of the palace. Rather than heading toward the gatehouse, ready to leave for the night, she went to the physicians' chamber. Before she could even knock, the door opened, and she was forced to jump back.

"Oh, Miss Scarlett," Morgan said in surprise as he stepped outside. "Walsingham said he had sent you out of the palace."

"No doubt he thought he had." Kit looked up and down the corridor, wary of Walsingham arriving and seeing her defying his orders. "I have to ask, Morgan."

"I know." Morgan scratched his head then stepped back through the doorway, leaving it open for her to move inside. Cautiously, she stepped in, her eyes flitting to the table where

Iomhar had been laid out. Her body turned cold when she saw it was empty.

"Do not tell me…" She trailed off, pulling at Morgan's cloak.

"He is alive." At his words, Kit let out a breath and released his cloak. "He needs rest. That is the only thing we can do now."

"You are telling me he is not out of danger, are you not?" she asked.

Morgan shifted, appearing a little guilty. "Through that door, you will find him. Stay with him if you like. I do not suppose you want Walsingham to know you are still here, and it is as good a place to hide as anywhere else." He nodded at her. "I judge him to be safe with you, Miss Scarlett. After all, you were right about that tonic you brought me to test."

"I was?" Kit said, barely able to concentrate on his words.

"Poison. Ratsbane. Small quantities. It would have made the queen deteriorate over time with the increasing amounts she took. If we had not been looking for it, it's possible we would have mistaken it for a natural death."

Kit felt sick at the mere idea. "Is there anything you can do for her?"

"She has a bezoar stone; we must rely on that and time. Goodnight, Miss Scarlett." Morgan bowed to her and left. Kit called after him with her thanks, but he moved so quickly she was unsure if he heard her.

Peering around the physicians' chambers, she checked none of the other men were there before creeping toward Iomhar's room and putting her head around the door. It was not much bigger than a cupboard. The bed was pushed against the wall, beneath a narrow window, and the covers were untidy across the straw mattress.

Kit tiptoed in further, wary of waking Iomhar, and closed the door behind her. With the light from the window fading, she had to feel her way through the shadows. She was careful not to walk into a table at the side of the room and felt for a chair that was thrust against a nearby wall. The room was so small that when she sat down, her feet could touch the side of the bed.

The creaking of the chair had to have alerted him in his sleep, for Iomhar moved on the bed. It was enough to reveal his face, which emerged from beneath the sheets. He still slept, his eyes tightly closed, and his lips parted as a soft snore escaped him.

Kit sat forward to try and see how he was doing in the dim light. He was wearing nothing on his chest and there were bruises across his shoulders. His skin was the hue of milk, and his hair was mussed from the hours spent lying down.

Beside him on the table was an empty tankard. Lifting it to her nose, Kit found the scent of flowers hanging in the air. It made her gag and replace the tankard on the table, wondering what they had fed him to try and make him well. She had a feeling she had smelt those flowers somewhere before, and that the fragrance had knocked her unconscious.

"That ye?"

Kit's head darted to Iomhar. His eyes fluttered open before they closed again.

"Iomhar?" she whispered, leaning toward him and reaching out to touch the edge of the bed. "Can you hear me?"

His lips pressed together, and no more words came. Whatever they had given him to drink must have made rousing quite difficult, for he appeared to be too weak to fight it. Though his eyes did not open, his hand moved toward the edge of the bed. Kit took it in hers, but the fingers went limp in her grasp and those soft snuffled snores began again. He could not be truly aware she was there, not in this state.

"Wake up soon," she murmured. "Please."

# CHAPTER 21

A tap on the door made Kit jerk forward. She cricked her neck, lifting a hand to soothe the ache and looking around to take stock of where she was. She had not left Iomhar's side all night and had fallen asleep in the chair beside him, with her head resting against the wall. When the tap on the door came again, she stretched her muscles, pushing her feet back into the boots she had kicked off overnight. Opening the door, she found Morgan beyond, peering in with his arms folded.

"It was a good place to hide, then," he said with a smile. "You were not found?"

"No. The physicians did not check on him," Kit said, realising she had not been disturbed all night.

"They are attending to the queen. There is not much more they can do for him." Morgan inched to Iomhar's side and reached down, placing his fingers on his wrist and measuring his pulse.

"What was in that tankard? It stinks," Kit said, watching what he was doing.

"Do not ask. A rare flower in these parts. It is good for making men sleep. That is what he needs to recover." Shifting his focus, Morgan peeled back the bedsheets from Iomhar's shoulders. Kit went to turn her head away to be respectful when she caught sight of the wound on Iomhar's side. It was a mess, with two different sets of stitches.

"This is…" Kit began, struggling for the right words.

"Untidy?" Morgan offered. "We had to be quick, that is the only excuse I can offer. We stopped the bleeding beneath the skin, at least. See, the bruising has calmed down." He pointed to where the skin had faded from purple to white. Kit looked away, lifting her gaze from Iomhar's wound to his face, feeling as if she was invading his privacy. "He was asking for you."

"I beg your pardon?" Kit said distractedly, keeping her eyes on Iomhar's face. He was still fast asleep.

"When we opened the wound up again. He was hardly best pleased, fighting against us. We had to hold him down." He gestured to the bruising on Iomhar's shoulders. "He called for you. He was quite upset to hear Walsingham had ordered you out of the palace."

"Well, Iomhar does not agree with everything Walsingham does," Kit said. "How does he fare this morning? Will he live?" She waited with bated breath for the answer.

Morgan placed the back of his hand on Iomhar's temple, checking his temperature before he stepped back. "I have every reason to think he will live."

Kit smiled but faltered, her eyes flicking back to the tankard. "Then why does he not wake up?"

"It is a strong thing," Morgan said, motioning to the tankard, "and his body could be keeping him asleep, the better to recover. Exhaustion, there is a reason for it."

Kit slumped down into the chair once more. The relief had made her body weak. "He will live," she murmured.

"I should think so. Now," Morgan turned to her, "you may have been able to hide here for the night, but I should not think you can hide here all day too. The physicians will come to see him at some point."

"Then I shall return to my task," Kit said, standing. She moved to the door. "If he wakes up, would you let me know?"

Morgan offered a sad smile. "I give you my word."

"Thank you." She turned away, hurrying out of the room.

Once she was in the corridor, she adjusted her posture, standing taller and flicking the collar of her doublet out, trying to set it straight. When she passed a window, she came to a hurried stop, finding her hair was as messy as her clothes. She ran her fingers through the locks, attempting to tame them, then pulled her hat from her pocket and thrust it on her head. She had barely completed her task when footsteps rounded the corner of the corridor, heading in her direction.

"Kit, you are back early," Walsingham said, his voice cold.

"You wished me to help with another search, did you not?" she asked, pushing her hands into her pockets.

"That I did. Go to the courtyard; you will find intelligencers there."

"Intelligencers? What of the guards?"

"They are making a poor job of the search. This time, only intelligencers will look, only men I trust." At his choice of words, Kit raised her eyebrows. "One woman, too. I still trust you, Kit, even if you doubt me. Now, head to the courtyard." He took her shoulder and hurried her away, in the direction of the nearest staircase. He was not so angry at her today, that was plain, but he also had not forgiven her for her mistrust.

Kit returned to the courtyard later that day, standing in the very middle and twisting her head back and forth. She and the intelligencers had searched the palace. It had been a slow task with fewer men, and none of them had offered up any new ideas on where the gunpowder could be hidden.

Frustrated, Kit was ready to start the search all over again by herself when a window was thrust open high above her in the courtyard and a lady began to wave a handkerchief in her direction. Flicking her head toward it, Kit saw it was Lady

Hunsdon, trying to get her attention. The lady beckoned her before shutting the window.

Looking around to see if anyone else had noticed the silent but urgent action, Kit returned into the building. She hastened through the corridors, the great hall and up the stairs, once more returning to the queen's chambers. Lady Hunsdon was waiting for her and hurrying her inside.

"What is happening?" Kit asked, to which Lady Hunsdon pressed a firm finger to her lips, being careful to close the door behind Kit as they walked into the room.

The privy chamber was eerily empty. There were no ladies in corners with handkerchiefs in their hands, fearing for their queen's life, and no ladies whispering gossip.

"Where is everyone?"

"I have sent them for food," Lady Hunsdon said, ushering Kit toward the withdrawing chamber. "It is the one chance I have had to be alone with the queen to discuss moving her."

"And? What has she said?"

Lady Hunsdon didn't reply but thrust the door open, then ushered Kit through the net curtain. The queen was more alert than before, not so prostrate on her pillows and even bearing a quilted shawl upon her shoulders. Her fingers shook as she held on to it. Lady Stafford sat in her nearly ever-present place beside her.

"Miss Scarlett?" the queen addressed her as she entered, her voice sounding much more like the voice Kit had first heard when she had seen the queen with her counsellors. "Lady Hunsdon tells me you wish to move me."

"Yes, Your Majesty."

"I wish to hear why."

"As I said, Your Majesty," Lady Hunsdon began, but the queen shot her a look.

"Anne, I heard your explanation. Now allow me to hear it from the woman who has saved my life." The words were quiet yet uttered with a power that brooked no refusal.

Lady Hunsdon nodded softly and moved to sit on the edge of the bed, allowing Kit to inch forward a little more as the queen returned her focus to her.

"I am relieved to see you have improved," Kit began cautiously. "It means such a proposal is possible."

"Improbable is the word I would have used." The queen leaned back on the pillows, as if the effort of speaking with such fervour was sapping her energy fast. She waved a hand at Lady Stafford, who passed her a small bottle. The queen hung her nose over the bottle, inhaling the sharp and pungent scent. It was so strong that Kit's eyes stung even from where she was standing, a foot away from the bed. "If you urge me to my feet, Miss Scarlett, I will quickly fall over. What good can come of that?"

"I would rather see you fall than stay here," Kit murmured. Her words shocked the three ladies present. The ladies-in-waiting turned their heads away and the queen sat forward once more, her lips curling as if she was both startled and amused by Kit's audacity. "There is gunpowder in this palace, Your Majesty. Walsingham and Lord Burghley can insist on as many searches as they like, but we are not able to find it. I suggest that wherever it is hidden is ingenious indeed."

"More ingenious than any of Walsingham's intelligencers?" the queen asked with a smirk. "Walsingham would dismiss such an idea."

"There will always be another cleverer person out there." Kit's mind flicked to Lord Ruskin, knowing he could still be close by. If he had managed to get into the palace once dressed as a yeoman guard, then it was possible he could return again.

"The man who intends to use the gunpowder has found one way to get into this palace already. If he returns and sees you leaving, then it is possible he will light the gunpowder."

"You are hardly encouraging me to leave," the queen laughed, but the sound was hollow.

"I wish to urge you to leave in disguise." Kit's words caught the queen's interest. She turned her head to Kit and lifted one eyebrow, bringing the sniffing bottle back to her nose. "It is the one way I can think of to keep you safe, Your Majesty."

The queen stayed silent for a minute, then beckoned Kit closer, until she was standing at the very edge of the bed. "Why do you go to such lengths for me, I wonder?" the queen asked. "There are many servants and intelligencers who aid me, but to this extent? That is a little rarer to find."

"It is my purpose."

"Your purpose? What an odd thing to say." The queen seemed intrigued. "Do you defend me out of your loyalty to Walsingham, Miss Scarlett? Or to me?"

"Both." Kit answered without hesitation, bringing another smile to the queen's face.

"An honest answer. I appreciate that." The queen reclined on the pillows, looking between her friends. "If we are to do this, then it cannot be tonight. I need sleep, much of it."

Sensing the queen was beginning to accept what had to be done, Kit stood taller, eager to speak of her plan. "May I suggest we offer tomorrow night at dusk? Darkness is always the best time to move, and by then we can organise a disguise for you."

"I hope you are not planning to bring me a hose and jerkin to wear." The queen waved her sniffing bottle in Kit's direction. "They may suit you, but I do not wish to wear them."

"They're surprisingly freeing, Your Majesty," Kit said, gesturing down to her legs. The genuine smile on the queen's face was a relief to see. She was indeed recovering, even if the process was a slow one.

"It is settled, then. Miss Scarlett will bring a disguise for me tomorrow evening."

"One more thing," Kit said, looking around the room. "Only we must know of this plan. None of the other ladies-in-waiting can know. From what I've seen they have a habit of gossiping, and we cannot risk others knowing."

"What of Walsingham?" the queen asked, arching an eyebrow.

"I will tell him." Kit knew she could not move the queen without telling Walsingham, even if the idea did not appeal to her. She wanted to trust him, though her heart wasn't in it at that moment.

# CHAPTER 22

"I will find something she can wear," Kit said formally to Walsingham as she walked alongside him.

"Good. Go to Seething Lane. Search the wardrobes and the coffers. I do not want a trail of purchases to be tracked by anyone who could be watching us." Walsingham spoke distractedly as he hurried down the corridor. In this part of the palace there were few windows, only slithers of light every now and then. It left their path dark and full of shadows, so that Kit could barely see where they were putting their feet.

They were heading toward a small chamber, tucked away in the corner of Hampton Court. Outside of the doorway and flanked by green tapestries stood a group of men, all dressed in black, some with their hair white and drawn back from their faces, others balding, and with the bristles greying along their chins. Lord Burghley was amongst them, gesturing toward Walsingham to hurry.

"What can a privy council discuss now?" Kit asked as Walsingham stopped walking. He nodded to Lord Burghley before turning to Kit.

"There is much to discuss. Constantly. With the queen incapacitated, there are matters of state. Lord Burghley is also insisting that we do more for the queen's safety."

"What more is there to do?" Kit's gaze flicked to Lord Burghley, seeing he was watching the two of them together with evident mistrust. He struck his cane against the floorboards.

"Do not ask him that," Walsingham said with a small amount of humour. "He will ask for the earth and heavens to be moved for him."

Kit could not smile with him. She turned her gaze back on Walsingham, narrowing her eyes in anger. He seemed to sense it, his smile vanishing.

"You look at me as if you hate me these days," Walsingham said.

"I am deciding whether to trust you or not."

"You trust me, Kit. Even if you do not wish to, you do."

Kit had a feeling he was right. Her stomach knotted, but she didn't walk away. She stayed exactly where she was, looking between him and Lord Burghley. "I want answers. Give me them and you will hear no more objections from me," she insisted.

Walsingham shook his head before she had even finished speaking. "You have become unruly these days. Wild. You begin to make me wonder if you can continue as an intelligencer at all."

"I am good at what I do for you."

"Are you?" he asked. "I need intelligencers that will not question my loyalty to the queen. Any more questioning of me, Kit, and I might find it is time I sent you away, somewhere far from London and Hampton Court, so that you might consider where your loyalties are."

He walked away abruptly, not giving her time to answer. Kit stared after him, her hands balled into fists.

When Walsingham reached Lord Burghley, the two were the first ones into the chamber, with the rest of the men following, all speaking so quickly and with such passion that it was evident their council meeting had begun before they had even sat down. Kit waited until the door closed, before she moved away.

Hastening through the corridor, she tried to concentrate on the sounds of her boots hitting the floorboards, but nothing could distract her. Her mind was too much on one thing. If Walsingham wished to send her away, that didn't sound so much like him questioning her own loyalties; it suggested he wanted to put distance between the two of them, as if he was worried about what she would ask next.

"He is hiding something from me. Of that, I have no doubt," she whispered to herself, marching through Hampton Court's corridors and out into the open air.

Kit strode through the house in Seething Lane with impatience, thrusting open wardrobes and coffers to search for clothes that had been discarded there over the years. She found gowns used by Lady Sidney that had been left behind after trips to see her father. Tempted by the idea of irking Lady Sidney by taking one, Kit's hand lingered over the material for a minute before she thrust the cupboard door closed once more. She decided she did not want to risk Lady Sidney's wrath.

She made such loud knocks and clatters opening and closing the cupboard doors that Doris soon appeared, poking her head through one of the doorways with her brows knitted together.

"Kitty?" the housekeeper exclaimed in surprise. "What a mess you are making! What are you doing?"

Kit paused and looked around the room to see that Doris was right. She had tossed some of the clothes across the nearest table, the better to see them and decide whether they would be good enough for the task ahead. At present, all the gowns were too fine to even consider taking.

"I am struggling, that is what I am doing," Kit said with difficultly and opened the next wardrobe beside her.

"I thought you said you had come to find something Walsingham needed?" Doris said, stepping into the room and picking up the gowns, trying to tidy up after Kit as she went.

"Well, he will certainly not be wearing it," Kit murmured, though Doris heard her, raising an eyebrow. At Kit's grimace, Doris nodded in understanding.

"Another one of the many secrets that come into this house that I am not allowed to know." She continued with her tidying.

The thought of secrets grabbed Kit's attention. She paused, one hand in the wardrobe and the other on the door as she looked at Doris. "I am sure you know many of Walsingham's secrets from over the years, Doris," Kit began slowly. "Perhaps you do not even realise what secrets they are."

"Ah, I know some of them," she said with a giggle and tapped her nose. She pushed one of the gowns into the nearest wardrobe, reaching for a discarded farthingale and trying to wrestle that one away too.

"How long have you been with Walsingham?" Kit asked, pulling out another gown. This was not as fine as the others, but still grander than Kit would have liked. If her plan was to work, she needed the queen to appear as a maid in her own palace.

"Must be these thirty years now," Doris said with a chuckle. "Had to keep the place proper for him when he was in Paris. That's when he was a young man, though. Not so welcome here in England under our last queen." She tutted at the mere mention of Queen Elizabeth's older sister, Queen Mary. "When he returned and took this house, he brought me here with him from his last abode. Such secrets in these walls, so many people coming and going in the shadows or in the night. Been an interesting time, I say."

Kit turned away from the wardrobe completely, moving her gaze to Doris with interest. "Doris, do you remember the day Walsingham brought me here?"

"How could I forget?" Doris said, picking up another of the gowns and flapping it out to remove the creases from the skirt. "Such a little thing you were."

"Was I?" Kit scrunched her nose, thinking hard of that day, but she could recall nothing. "How old? If you were to guess, how old do you reckon I was?"

"I should say…" Doris paused, folding the gown up as she thought hard, her tongue pressed between her teeth. "About three. Maybe even two. Had a mouth on you, though, for one that was so young. You liked to talk. That accent, too — you certainly lost that quick once Walsingham started your lessons."

"Accent?" Kit moved away from the wardrobe. She inched toward Doris, placing her hands down on the table between them, staring at her. "What kind of accent?"

"You sounded like Mr Blackwood. Well, a little, certainly not the same accent, but similar."

"Scottish?" Kit spluttered in surprise, finding herself reaching for the nearest chair and turning it round to sit down.

"Possibly. I cannot be certain, Kitty, but it was similar." Doris's words fell on deaf ears. Kit was too busy staring at the stretched-out gowns between them, trying to make sense of what she had heard.

To have an accent even remotely similar to Iomhar's, she had to have been born very far away, spending her early years somewhere in the north, perhaps in Scotland itself. Such a history did not fit with Walsingham's tale of her pulling on his cloak as a beggar child in a back lane of London.

"Has the master not told you this?" Doris asked, reaching for another gown.

"No, never." Kit lifted her gaze from the gowns, chewing her lip. "Is there anything else you can remember from that day?"

"Let's see…" Doris thrust the gown into a coffer and reached for muslin caps, taking one at a time and bundling them together into a pile. "You would barely let go of the master; I remember that. He had you swaddled in his cloak, like you were made of some fine silver." She chuckled at the idea, reminiscing in a rather wistful tone. "The gown you wore too, that was interesting."

"Gown?" Kit repeated, leaning forward and longing to know more.

"It was rather fine, I thought, with pearls along your neck."

Kit lifted a hand and trailed a finger along the neckline of her doublet, remembering well enough where she had seen such a thing before. It was in her dream under the water.

"What of the colour? Do you remember the colour of the gown?" Kit's mind shot back to the pink silk she had seen.

"Too long ago to remember, Kitty. Is it important?" Doris asked.

"No, not very," Kit lied, trying to hide how interested she was. "Walsingham always told me I pulled on his cloak in the street, as a beggar child."

"I have heard him say the same. I always presumed you must have been abandoned there by your real parents, Kitty," Doris said with a pitying tone as she went to tidy away the last of the stays and chemises. "It would explain the rather fine gown and the accent if you came from elsewhere."

"Yes, I suppose so." Kit stood and returned to the coffers.

"Oh, must we take them all out again? It was all so tidy." Doris huffed and placed her hands on her hips.

"Has Walsingham ever said anything else to you? About where I came from?" Kit asked distractedly, reaching into the bottom of the coffer and pulling out a plain white linen dress. This one was not like the others but poor and even tatty, with the hem torn and the bodice loose. She held it up to the sunlight that streamed through the windows. If she could persuade the queen to dress in such a way, there was no chance of her being recognised.

"Not that I can remember," Doris said, tutting once more as Kit sifted through the muslin caps, accidentally tossing a couple to the floor. "He always looked rather haunted, though."

"Haunted?" Kit whispered as she paused with a muslin cap in one hand.

"You will need this too, Kitty." Doris pressed some stays into her hand along with a woollen shawl, the type that was poor and thin, barely offering any warmth at all.

"You said haunted, Doris?" Kit urged her.

"Oh yes." Doris nodded, picking up the dropped caps and returning them to their place. "I quickly realised it was not a conversation to be had. You were here to stay, and that was the end of the matter. Never mind how you got here in the first place. Now, is that all you need?"

"Shoes," Kit murmured, her voice rather weakened by the surprise.

"Let me see what we can find." As Doris turned away to hunt down some shoes, Kit stood perfectly still, staring down at the gown, cap and shawl in her grasp. It seemed there were more secrets about how she'd been brought here. Whether her dream was real or not, Walsingham wouldn't even trust his own housekeeper with the secret, let alone Kit. "Who are these for, Kitty?" Doris asked, turning back and passing her a pair of soft-soled shoes.

"Someone who is in need of them. That is all I can say." Kit thanked her heartily and left the room in a hurry. As she parted from Seething Lane, she tucked the clothes under her arm and walked as though she were numb, barely taking note of the things and the people that were around her. She was too busy thinking of the hint of her past that Doris had given her.

# CHAPTER 23

"Lady Hunsdon?" Kit called from across the privy chamber. The lady turned, her eyes moving over Kit before she marked the clothes that were tucked under her arm. Taking the hint, she turned back to the ladies and ushered them together with a wave of her arm.

"Ladies, I think it is time we gathered around our queen. Blanche, perhaps you could share a song with us? One of those ditties you are so good at. They do well at cheering her spirits." Lady Hunsdon spoke with flattery, urging the women to their feet and into the withdrawing chamber. The distraction worked perfectly, for Lady Hunsdon was able to hover back in the privy chamber, waiting for them all to depart before she hurried to Kit's side and held out her arms for the clothes.

"For the queen to wear tonight," Kit whispered. "How will you ensure the ladies are distracted?"

"I will send them for their supper late tonight," Lady Hunsdon said. "They will never question it." She paused, her eyes flitting down to the clothes in her grasp. "You expect our queen to wear *these*? They are a pauper's clothes!"

"Yes, but tonight she must be a pauper if she wishes to live."

Lady Hunsdon stood taller and stuffed the clothes firmly beneath her arm. "You are an audacious one, Miss Scarlett."

"I think the queen's pride can suffer for one evening if it means she escapes this place, do you not agree?" Kit asked, watching as Lady Hunsdon closed her lips together. "Yes, that is what I thought. This evening Walsingham and I will come to collect her. You must follow closely behind."

"Where is it we are going?"

"To the stables of Richmond Palace. From there, you will travel together to Hatfield House."

"Hatfield?" Lady Hunsdon repeated in surprise. "You wish Her Majesty to leave London?"

"Yes." Kit had discussed it at length with Walsingham before he'd gone into his council meeting, and they had agreed it was for the best. So far from London, it would be harder for Lord Ruskin and his friends to find out where she was.

Lady Hunsdon appeared ready to argue once more before thinking better of it, glancing down at the clothes. "Very well," she agreed. "Then do not be late. She will not take kindly to wearing such clothes for long." As Lady Hunsdon hurried off, Kit stifled a smile. How the queen felt about her disguise was the least of her worries; there were greater matters to concern her.

Turning away and stepping out of the door, Kit took up her post by the gentlemen-at-arms as the sound of running feet in the corridor caught her attention. It was Morgan, his thin shoes clattering against the boards so loudly that the gentlemen-at-arms stepped forward with their hands on their weapons belts, alerted to the urgency.

"Morgan? What is wrong?" Kit asked, moving in front of the guards.

"Miss Scarlett," Morgan panted, recovering from his run. "You wished to be told ... as soon as he was awake."

Kit did not wait for another word. She pushed past him, running faster than he had done to reach her. She nearly tripped more than once as she climbed a spiral staircase, reaching the landing on which the physicians' chambers were placed.

At the physicians' door, she didn't knock but pushed it open and stepped in, startling the physician who was at the table. He spilled some of the ale from his tankard down his doublet, the liquid dribbling from his lips.

"Morgan? What is this?" the physician called through the open doorway.

Morgan arrived a few seconds after Kit. "Miss Scarlett wished to be told when the patient was awake."

She let them have their conversation and turned to the door beyond which she knew Iomhar was being kept. Thrusting it open, she stepped inside and then squealed in surprise.

"Aye, good to see ye too, Kit," Iomhar said with a strained smile as he pulled a shirt over his head. She looked away, trying to give him the privacy he needed. "I'm decent now. Ye can turn back." Kit whipped round to find that Iomhar was standing but leaning on the bedhead. "I do not think I have ever seen ye blush so much."

"Well, at least you are jesting again," she said with a smile and hurried further into the room. She reached for his arm first, needing some contact, though she was unsure how to show it. Unlike her, Iomhar did not hesitate. He turned and lifted his hand from the bedhead, drawing her into an embrace.

Kit's eyes widened within his arms. This was not something they normally did, yet her hands clutched his loose shirt, finding she needed that touch. They both stood there in silence for a minute.

"Ahem." Morgan's voice from the doorway made Kit step back, releasing Iomhar's shirt, though he seemed in less of a hurry to release her, his hands moving to her arms instead as he shot a look Morgan's way. Kit turned toward the apothecary, hoping to hide the extent of her blush. She could feel it burning all the way up into the roots of her hair.

"How is he?" she asked Morgan.

"He will be fine. I would rather he rested for longer, but getting him to stay in that bed is like telling a frog to sit still. He will not listen."

Kit flicked her eyes to Iomhar, seeing that he was still pale. Despite the hours of sleep there was a darkness under his eyes, and his hair was unruly.

"How are you feeling?" Kit asked, stepping back enough so that Iomhar's hands dropped from her arms.

"I am fine," he said, his voice insistent. Yet as he took a step forward, he wobbled on his feet, having to reach out and take hold of the bedhead once more. Kit moved forward, her hand going for his arm to keep him standing. He seemed to smile at that touch. "Planning to catch me if I fall over?"

"Maybe I will just push you back on that bed instead," she said with a smirk. "You do not look well."

"That is what I told him," Morgan agreed.

"I am well. Aye, I am better than I was, am I not?" Iomhar asked.

"True, you are awake at least, and you are no longer making those snuffling sounds." She gestured to his face, watching as he lifted his brows.

"Ye were here as I was sleeping? Odd, I thought I dreamt that."

"You said her name enough times in your sleep," Morgan observed with humour, drawing a darker look from Iomhar.

"Thank ye for that." His tone deepened as Morgan stepped away.

"Miss Scarlett, see if you can persuade him to stay here longer. He will not listen to me." Morgan retreated into the main chambers, leaving the door open behind him.

Kit shifted her focus back to Iomhar, seeing that he could barely hold his body straight. "He is right, Iomhar," she said, her voice gentle. "You are not in a fit state to leave this bed."

"Tell me, is there not gunpowder somewhere in this palace?" he whispered sternly. "Ye wish me to stay in this room when it could explode at any second?"

"You are far enough away from the queen's rooms that I think it unlikely you would be hurt here," Kit said hurriedly. "Besides, you can barely walk."

"I can walk fine." Iomhar released the bedhead and tried to move past her. He only took three steps, trying to reach for his boots as he fell into the nearest wall, flattening his palms against it. Kit chased after him, collecting him quickly and pushing him toward the bed.

"Yes, you are right, that is a completely normal manner in which to walk." Kit released him once he was sitting on the bed and stood firmly in front of him with her arms folded, refusing to let him stand again.

"Ye realise I could just push ye out of my way?" he said with amusement, earning a laugh from her.

"In your state? I fancy my chances in a fight against you for a change."

"All I need is food, Kit."

"Then eat." She pushed his shoulder, urging him back onto the bed. He didn't move at first, prompting her to be more forceful. At last, he did as she asked, and she nearly fell over him in her effort to stand straight again. She ended up sitting on the bed, facing him as he sank back against the bedhead, his body exhausted. "You need your rest, Iomhar. Tell me the truth." Kit paused, chewing her lip as she glanced down at the shirt he was wearing. "How bad is it?" She pointed at the wound.

"They say I will recover. I do not wish to tell ye how sore it is," he said, holding her gaze. Kit slapped his arm on his good side, making him wince. "Ow, what was that for?"

"You are not to do it again!"

"Do what?"

"You are not to step in front of a blade for me again."

"I cannot make that promise," Iomhar said with a small smile. When she hit his arm again, he laughed through his wince. "Kit, I will never make ye that promise."

"God's wounds!" she muttered, ready to tell him off another time when there was a tap at the door.

Morgan had reappeared and was sticking his head through the doorway. "Miss Scarlett, Walsingham is here. He says it is time."

The words made Kit's smile vanish. She nodded slowly and turned to Iomhar, finding him watching her closely.

"What is it time for?" he asked quietly.

"We are going to get her out of here," Kit whispered.

"Then let me help." Iomhar jerked forward, but Kit pushed him back.

"You will stay here."

"I still think I could push past ye."

"Would you like to try?" she asked.

Iomhar seemed to think the better of it and sat back. "I've had enough injuries," he muttered. Kit stood, glancing toward the doorway. Unable to part just yet, she reached for Iomhar. She went for his shoulder, but his hand met hers in the middle instead, his fingers grasping hers. "Aye, I am well, Kit. Don't worry about me."

"I will be back tonight."

"Good. I'd rather ye were here than I just dreamt of ye again."

Kit wanted to ask what he meant by that, but Morgan was clearing his throat with urgency. She offered Iomhar one last smile before she left.

"I look like a maid," complained the queen.

"That is the idea." Kit's quiet reply was met with a dark stare from the beady eyes beneath the muslin cloth. Kit had abandoned her usual address of 'Your Majesty'. If their plan was to work, then they could offer no hint of who was really beneath the muslin cap.

Kit stepped slowly through the great hall, heading toward the door at the far end, with the queen's arm linked firmly through her own. The queen was so weak that she struggled to walk at all, so Kit was taking most of her weight. The only one that followed them was Walsingham, turning his gaunt face back and forth as he checked the hall.

"What madness this is," the queen muttered as they stepped out of the rooms and through a door into the courtyard. "I like to think I would be recognised by all my people, no matter what I wore."

"I pray tonight you are wrong," Kit whispered, searching the courtyard with quick eyes before she even considered leading the queen forward. The courtyard was almost dark. An evening mist hung over the russet rooftops of the palace, hiding the many chimneys from view. Shadows obscured the doorways, meaning that anyone could be skulking in the corners, watching them.

"We are ready," Walsingham said, reaching their side. "Straight through the gatehouse." He gestured to the gate up ahead. "I have arranged a carriage for you."

"A carriage?" Kit said in surprise as she led the queen forward. The moment she heard the words, she was on edge.

No maid would travel in a fine carriage. They would have been better off arranging for a horse and cart. "Better she travel with hay as a companion than in a fine carriage."

"Some respect you show for your queen, Miss Scarlett," the queen spoke with derision.

"I have the greatest respect for you. You may have noticed that I am trying to keep you alive," Kit replied, seething. She silenced herself when the queen turned a glare upon her.

"This is not the time for arguments," Walsingham said sharply. "We must go." He led the way through the courtyard. When Kit began to struggle with the queen's weight, she had to whistle at Walsingham. He hurried to their side and took the queen's other arm, hoisting her up higher. Between the two of them, they were able to move her much faster, with the soft-soled shoes she was forced to wear slipping repeatedly on the dewy surface of the cobblestones.

They passed under the arched gatehouse that was manned by yeomen, who were barely taking any interest in a maid walking with Walsingham and Kit. Beyond the small bridge that connected the drive to the gatehouse, the carriage awaited them. The closer they moved toward it, the more Kit slowed her pace.

It was a fine carriage indeed. She felt anger stir at the sight. In Walsingham's attempt to pander to the queen's wishes, he had endangered her.

"Kit, why are you slowing?" Walsingham demanded.

"Because *this* was not the idea," Kit said, bringing them to a complete stop and gesturing to the carriage. The queen was too tired to fight her and leant upon her shoulder.

Walsingham could not drag them both, so he turned to face them, his white face contorted like a stone gargoyle's. "Move to the carriage, Kit. Now."

Kit flicked her eyes to the carriage, noting that the driver had descended from it. He was so busy attending to the horses' reins that he didn't notice a shadow passing behind him.

"Wait," Kit ordered, her voice so harsh that Walsingham froze, those eyes narrowing further. "There is someone there."

"It will be the footman."

The shadow moved off from the carriage, running away from it so quickly that he left Kit in no doubt that he was not a footman.

"No, it is no footman. Get back." Kit shoved the queen behind her. She nearly fell over, gripping Kit's wounded arm so tightly that she gritted her teeth at the pain.

"Kit, have you lost your good sense?" Walsingham snapped.

Kit barely had time to reach for Walsingham's arm and shove him further back as the hiss reached her ears. Something was burning...

"Cover your ears and hide!" she ordered.

"What in God's name —"

Walsingham didn't have time to finish his curse, for the carriage exploded.

# CHAPTER 24

The glow was so strong that it blurred Kit's vision. Shards of wood were shooting into the air, and now flames were leaping out of the carriage, each one as tall as a man.

The queen fell back from behind Kit, dropping to the floor as a scream erupted from her mouth.

Kit could see Walsingham out of the corner of her eye. Like her, he was staring at the carriage, his eyes so wide that the flames were reflected in the whites.

"That could have been…"

"Do not say it," Kit begged, turning round. She put her back to the fire, aware that the poor coach driver was undoing the horses as best he could. One of the horses was singed, but the rest were merely spooked, running away as fast as they could.

Kit reached down to the queen and took her hand, hauling her to her feet before she could complain. No further sound escaped her, but her face had become a picture of pure fear, her lips trembling.

"Kit?" Walsingham called. Kit thrust the queen toward him, demanding in silence that he help her. "How did they know?"

"The carriage," she said firmly. "If you order a carriage as fine as that, only one person is going to be driven away from this palace, are they not?" Her words struck Walsingham deeply. She could see the guilt and horror clearly, the realisation that it was his order that had nearly killed the queen. "We need to get her inside."

Kit thrust the queen back past the yeomen guards that were jumping forward, trying to see what they could do to stop the flames. Each time Kit urged the queen on, she fought against it. Already weakened by her illness, her fear had now frozen her to the spot.

"Your Majesty, you must move!" Walsingham insisted.

"Must I?" the queen asked, outraged. "The last time I was ordered to do something by the two of you, I nearly walked into a burning carriage!"

"Staying out here will not keep you safe." Walsingham's words seemed to break her. She stopped fighting against Kit's thrusts and allowed herself to be dragged forward, across the courtyard and toward her chambers.

"What happens now?" the queen asked, her voice high-pitched with panic. "What do we do now? I cannot stay here. I cannot stay in this place!" As they reached the door, she placed her foot against the wall, trying to stop herself from being pushed inside.

"You must," Kit begged. "Whoever set off that gunpowder will be watching our movements. If we try to get you out of here again, they will be there. They will probably place gunpowder in every cart, carriage, and horse's saddle that leaves here." Her words made the queen whimper as Walsingham's free hand came up to tap Kit around the head. "Ow, what is it?"

"That detail is not helping."

"If it makes her go into the palace, then yes, it has helped."

The queen capitulated, lowering her foot and allowing Kit to draw her inside. They traipsed through the corridors and into the great hall, where they were met by Lady Hunsdon and the other ladies running their way, all as spooked as the horses had been by the explosion.

"What has happened?" Lady Hunsdon cried, reaching out to take the queen. She fell into her arms, hiding her face upon her friend's shoulder and crying. Many of the other ladies gathered round, all panicking and wondering why the queen was dressed as she was.

Amongst the outpouring of fear, Kit hurried to the window at the far end of the room, peering into the darkness. Over the rooftop, she could see the smoke billowing from the carriage. Whoever had placed the gunpowder there had intended for it to be blown to splinters, and nothing more.

Yet something was odd. Had the person truly intended to blow the queen up when she stepped into the carriage, they could have waited a few more seconds. He'd been almost too eager in his task. If he had stayed hidden behind the carriage, lighting his thread as they were climbing in from the other side, he could have achieved his aim.

Walsingham walked to Kit's side, his face blackened by the explosion. He rubbed it in agitation, then froze when he peered through the window, staring at the smoke.

"He was too quick," Walsingham said, echoing Kit's thoughts.

She nodded, shifting her focus to him. "He could have killed her had he lit that flame a few seconds later."

"Then … he did not intend for her to be inside?"

"He intended to scare her." Kit gestured back to where the queen was practically being carried by her ladies, lost in the throes of her fears as tears escaped down her cheeks. She pulled at the muslin cap and threw it from her head. "He intended to send her back into the palace." Kit didn't need to say any more to persuade Walsingham.

He stepped forward, blocking the ladies' path before they could take the queen to her chambers.

"Take Her Majesty to a guest chamber."

"I beg your pardon?" Lady Hunsdon cried in outrage.

Lady Hardwick stepped forward, her hands on her hips and her jaw agape. "The queen does not sleep anywhere else." Her voice shook with alarm.

"She does tonight." Walsingham's voice was firm. "If that explosion was designed to drive her back into the palace, then we cannot do what they will expect of us."

"Lady Hunsdon?" Kit called, waiting until the woman turned to look at her. "Trust us. Take her to your chamber, a guest chamber, anywhere but her own."

Lady Hunsdon nodded hurriedly, deciding not to argue further. When Lady Hardwick opened her mouth, Lady Hunsdon waved a hand in her direction, silencing her. "We do as they ask. Come, Your Majesty, let us find you a bed." She held on to her friend, pulling her up the few steps that led out of the great hall, with all the ladies-in-waiting following. For a long time after they'd left, their voices could be heard down the corridor, irate and incredulous.

When they were far enough away to be out of earshot, Kit turned to Walsingham. His shoulders were hunched, his hands were pressed against the nearest wall for support and his eyes were on the floor.

"What do we do next?" Walsingham asked, unable to lift his eyes to Kit. "I didn't think they'd watch the carriages. Every time we search for this gunpowder, we cannot find it. Now we cannot even get the queen out of here? She will be killed on the road, as if she were a common street thief! No, this cannot happen."

"Then we search. Again." Kit's firm voice prompted him to lift his gaze.

"You have searched. We all have. Many times."

"We do not give up now." Kit headed for the same corridor the ladies had walked down, though she did not intend to follow them. Pausing in the doorway, she looked back at Walsingham. "The man who set off the powder in that carriage could have been Lord Ruskin, or it could have been someone who works for him. We need to search the estate. Send the yeomen guards, send anyone."

"What of the search within the palace?" Walsingham asked, looking to her for the orders. Kit moved from foot to foot for a second, startled at the shift that had occurred between them.

"I will do it. Send the gentlemen-at-arms too, and we will search every crevice we can find, but there is somewhere very particular we must search first."

"Where is that?"

"The queen's chambers, and every room that meets them. Whether they share a wall, a ceiling, or just the corner of a wall. *That* is their target." Kit turned to walk away when Walsingham called after her.

"The king's apartments."

"What of them?" she asked, still walking.

Walsingham followed her. "They are beneath the queen's. Old King Henry's apartments have been locked for years." Walsingham's words brought Kit to a stop. Flicking her head round, she found him staring at her from the doorway, his lips parted in fear. "No one has been in there for decades, Kit. How could anyone get in there now?"

"The key?" she asked slowly.

"I believe the queen has it," he answered. "It is locked away. It is a rule of hers — no one could even find the key."

"We do not always need keys to open doors, Walsingham," Kit said. "I will search Her Majesty's chambers first. Find me the key for old King Henry's rooms. If whoever set light to that carriage is already within the palace's walls, then we do not have long. He will know we're looking for any way possible to get her out of here now."

"You mean ... tonight? He will light the gunpowder tonight?"

"I would wager everything I own." As she strode away, Walsingham hurried to catch up with her, keeping pace at her side.

Kit had examined every nook and cranny in the queen's rooms. She had even searched the coffers and the hiding place where the queen kept her secret ring, bearing the miniature of her mother. No matter what corner she searched, it was as empty of gunpowder as the last.

In the withdrawing chamber, Kit opened the makeup pots, even emptying creams and powders to see if any gunpowder remained at the bottom. She upturned chairs to check for secret panels in the floor and boards that could be lifted, but there was nothing. She raised the tapestries and pressed her head into the darkness, feeling with her fingers for doors in the walls, but there was nothing.

Soon, the darkness had grown so great that she had to light another candle to aid her search. It was tall but burned quickly. Pushing the candle out in front of her, she reached for the queen's bed and searched underneath it, but it was as empty as the last time she had looked. She stopped only when she heard footsteps in the doorway, recognising the sound of Walsingham's gait even before she looked up.

"Here." He hurried toward her and proffered a key. "You will find the rooms below this. The door is still marked with his letters and a broken pomegranate."

"Broken?" Kit said in surprise.

"One of the symbols of his first wife. It seems they did a poor job when trying to remove any trace of her. I must go; I will guard the queen's door with every other man. Come to me if you find anything."

"I give you my word." Kit was on her feet, finishing her search of the room as she thrust the key into her pocket.

As Walsingham left, there was no more questioning about loyalties. They both had tasks, and Walsingham was addressing his with such speed that Kit was beginning to think herself a fool for ever doubting him. Once he was gone, she took one last look around the room and left, heading to the rooms on either side first.

She found guards' rooms that were empty, for all the yeomen had been moved elsewhere. There were upturned tankards that had been dropped in surprise during the explosion and chairs that had been overturned as the guards had run to the door. Kit traced their paths across the room, seeing the signs of their hurried exit. There were scratches on the tables from which weapons belts had been snatched up, as well as residues of gunpowder from powder flasks.

Kit pressed the pad of her finger to the gunpowder, lifting it high so that she could see it in the candlelight, whilst being careful not to place it too near to the flame. It was tiny and innocuous, so black that it resembled the soot from a fire, apart from the silverish glow. The way it shone a little in the light was the only feature that helped her recognise it for what it really was.

Blowing the powder off her fingers so that it scattered across the table, she reached for the pistol that she had taken from Lord Ruskin, wondering where he would keep his gunpowder for the weapon. Any powder flask had to have a soft lining within the metal or wooden shell, to protect it from the chance of a spark. This made Kit consider how else Lord Ruskin could have snuck the powder into the palace.

A great number of barrels would have surely been noticed, especially if they had been bound with ropes to avoid sparks, but other vessels would not have raised so many eyebrows. Boxes and coffers that had been lined with wool could fulfil the task and enter the palace under the guise of delivered materials for the queen.

With this in mind, Kit hurried to the staircase that took her down toward the king's rooms. She went past the physicians' chambers, thinking of Iomhar beyond before running forward once more. She couldn't afford to dally if she was going to stop the inevitable explosion.

She reached the corridor of the king's rooms and found the very symbol Walsingham had spoken of. Lifting the candle to a timber archway pressed close to the wall, she found the etching of a firm H, and beside it, flanked by vines that wove together, there was what remained of a pomegranate, practically chipped in half.

A sound in the corridor made Kit lift her head, jerking the candle away from the symbol. Ahead of her, the darkness of the corridor was so thick that the single flame barely broke through. Inching forward, she waited to see if anyone would appear.

At first, there was nothing, only more shadows. Releasing a breath, Kit reached down to her weapons belt, curling her fingers around the hilt of one of her daggers. She grasped it for a second as she crept forward, waiting to see if one of the shadows would move.

When nothing did, she moved forward with more purpose, but her louder footsteps were answered by more sounds further down the corridor, and she came to a quick stop, thrusting the candle high over her head. She nearly called, to see if it was a yeoman guard that had come to search and act as a sentry, but the words died on her tongue as the light fell onto a silhouette.

In the doorway that led to the king's chambers, there was a figure leaning against the wood. Kit pulled one of the daggers from her belt and advanced. The sound of the blade scraping out of the scabbard made the figure jerk their head upward.

Kit cursed under her breath, trying to stay as quiet as possible. Someone was there, waiting in the shadows, trying to get into the rooms directly beneath the queen's chambers.

# CHAPTER 25

Darting forward with her hand outstretched, Kit pushed the dagger ahead of her as the stranger flattened themselves into the doorway.

"Who are you?" Kit demanded, just as the light of the candle fell on the man's face. She jerked the dagger back.

"I have enough injuries, Kit, please do not give me another," Iomhar said, holding his palms up.

"Iomhar? Dear God!" She hurried to push the blade back into the scabbard and dropped the candle onto a nearby ledge. "What are you doing here?"

"Making your heart stop dead, by the looks of things," he said, gesturing to her as she caught her breath. "Ye well?"

"Me? You are the one out of your sickbed."

"Aye, I am fine."

"Iomhar, you are clinging to the door behind you for dear life." Kit stood straight, placing a hand to her sternum as she breathed deeply. In the dim orange light, Iomhar's face did not look as pale as it had done earlier, but he was scruffier than usual. His doublet had been pulled hurriedly over his shoulders, and the laces were skewwhiff. Even one of his boots was not fastened properly.

"Why are ye here?"

"Searching." Kit fished in her pockets and pulled out the key for the room, pointing to the door. "Care to tell me why you are not in your sickbed?"

"The explosion," Iomhar muttered, his voice growing deeper and darker. "Wrenched me from eating stew, I can tell ye, and the physicians hurried out of the room, in case they were needed. Morgan wasn't so interested in the idea of stopping me from leaving then." Kit fought her smile, knowing how much smaller Morgan was than Iomhar. He had probably decided it was not worth the challenge. "After the explosion, there were some noises on these stairs." He gestured to the staircase she had just come down.

"Wait…" Kit murmured, thinking through what he was saying. "You heard someone come this way?"

"Aye, and this appears to be the only room here." He tapped the door he was leaning on. "Who set off the explosion?"

"It was nothing but a shadow." Kit tried to urge Iomhar to the side so she could push the key into the lock, but he seemed to struggle to move. "It could have been Lord Ruskin, but in truth, I do not know. You need to move a little more than that."

"It is not so easy to do." He grimaced as he shifted to the side. Kit paused and looked up at him, her teeth gritting together when she saw how much pain he was in. A muscle was twitching in his jaw beneath the unusually unkempt beard, and his eyes were turned away from her.

"You could have died, Iomhar."

"I know, Kit. I know."

"You cannot do it again." Her words made him turn his head toward her, revealing a small smile, despite the pain he was in.

"I told ye I cannot make that promise."

She wanted to argue with him, to insist that him stepping before that blade was a foolish thing to do, but it hardly seemed the right time. She turned her focus to the closed door, looking down at where she had pushed the key into the lock. Seeing there were scratches in the wood, she dropped to her knees for a closer look. Iomhar reached for the candle, wincing as he lifted it toward her so that the light fell on the lock.

"Look at these marks," she murmured.

"Aye, someone has been picking the lock. With a lock this old, I shouldn't think it a difficult thing to do."

Kit stood again and turned the key, pressing her finger to her lips. If someone was in that room as Iomhar suspected, then she didn't want to warn them they were coming. He nodded, showing he understood.

Slowly, she opened the door, freezing when it began to creak. Reluctant to make any more noise, she slipped through the narrow gap between the door and the frame. Iomhar followed her, though he was a little clumsier. Judging from the way his fingers had tightened around the brass candle holder, turning the knuckles white, Kit could see how much pain the movement had caused him. She went to help him, taking his arm. He leaned on her, whispering in her ear.

"If someone is here, ye release me and defend yourself."

"Only if you agree not to step in the way of the blade again," she insisted quietly, noting that he did not agree with her. When she attempted to release him, he stumbled, stretching out a hand to the nearest wall. "Iomhar, you must agree this is foolish. What good will you be if we meet Lord Ruskin?"

"I will find the strength if needed. Believe me," he said.

Kit looked away, not doubting him at all. She turned her focus to the room. It was larger than she had expected, and certainly broader than the first of the queen's private chambers. She inched forward, moving on her toes so that the heels of her boots would not make a sound. Iomhar followed her, though she suspected he moved so slowly out of necessity rather than an attempt to be quiet. As he raised the candle an inch higher, the light cascaded further across the room, revealing the far corners of everything there.

The room had clearly remained untouched for years. There was a vast table in the middle, bordered with four oak chairs that were exquisitely carved, though they were now caked in dust. Each nook within the carvings was filled with dust. Kit imagined spiders nestled within, waiting to appear.

Stepping past the table, she shifted her eyes toward the far end of the room. There was one great window, either side swathed with tapestries woven in red and the boldest of greens. Kit walked toward them, inching past the window to observe the embroidered faces.

"Haunting, is it not?" Iomhar whispered. She nodded in agreement, wanting to move away as quickly as possible.

When the floorboards creaked beneath Kit, she fell still, with Iomhar's hand reaching out for her arm, stilling her before she could make another sound. They exchanged a fearful look as another noise reached their ears.

It came from beyond a door in the corner of the room. The door was so large that it could have fitted a carriage through it, horses and all, with the brass handle glinting in the candlelight. When something clicked again, Iomhar released Kit, hurrying her forward.

She reached the door and turned the handle as slowly as she could, trying her best to make no sound. It still creaked no matter what she did, so she pressed her ear against it, waiting to see if another sound would come. Within seconds, it did. Someone was moving quickly around the room.

"Well?" Iomhar mouthed.

"Someone," Kit whispered, tilting her head in the direction of the door.

Iomhar lifted the candle and blew out the flame with no warning, casting the two of them into darkness. Kit would have preferred to see who was ahead of her when she opened the door, but Iomhar moved to her side, coming so close that she was silenced before she could voice her objection to the lack of light.

"We do not want them to know we are here," he whispered. Kit reached into her belt and pulled out the dagger, hearing that Iomhar was also reaching for a weapon. It was his crossbow. He clearly intended to avoid the pistol altogether, since they were about to enter a room possibly filled with gunpowder. She heard him preparing the crossbow, shifting the bolt within the frame, as her eyes adjusted to the darkness. With the moon firmly behind the clouds, it was almost impossible to see. She could merely trace the outline of Iomhar's head and the crossbow protruding forward, before she turned back to the door handle.

"Now," she whispered, aware that the steps on the other side of the door had gone quiet.

Pulling open the door, she let Iomhar step in first, his crossbow lifted before him, though he still walked at an odd angle because of his wound. The moment he stepped forward, Kit could see more thanks to a candle in the room, casting them in an amber glow. Craning her neck to look around Iomhar, she found they were in the king's withdrawing chamber, where only the closest of friends would have been permitted.

Here, the furniture was not so formal. The chairs showed signs of use and comfort, with some of the cushions heavily embroidered and worn down to the wood beneath. At the sides of the chamber, there were wardrobes and between two of these was a narrow door, which Kit suspected led to a garderobe.

In the middle of this space and atop a standing candelabra made of wrought iron were three candles. Each one had wax beading at the edges, with those drips running down the stems like tears, and flames were flickering on top. The light they bled around the room was bright, revealing that no one was here with them, yet a door was open on the other side.

Iomhar stepped forward first with Kit moving alongside him, her gaze flicking around the chamber to the coffers and boxes between the wardrobes. At first, she thought there was no sign of gunpowder, no barrels at all — then she noticed the furniture in detail. There was a settle bench where the seat was lifted slightly, revealing a dark space beneath. Feeding into this space was a thin twine of rope.

Pulling on Iomhar's sleeve, she urged him to stop and gestured toward the settle bench. He nodded and held his ground with the crossbow pointed toward the open door that led to the king's chamber, allowing Kit the minute she needed to step closer to the settle bench.

Peering in through the gap, she found the inner casement of the bench was filled with gunpowder, those silver filings glowing in the slip of candlelight. Backing up, she followed where the rope went with an outstretched finger. It connected more than one piece of furniture in that room, each piece looking newer than the older pieces, for they were free of the dust and cobwebs that adorned the king's original furniture.

The rope stretched between a coffer, a bible box, and even an oak cupboard, with its doors not quite shut and each drawer slightly open for the rope to be passed inside. Kit slowly opened one of these drawers, seeing that it was lined thickly with wool and filled with gunpowder. She shuddered at the sight, for the culprit had been both clever and careful.

Kit became aware of Iomhar waving an arm in her direction, trying to get her attention. Stepping over the intertwined ropes that wove a path around the withdrawing chamber like a labyrinth, she slipped between them all, not making a sound and reaching his side quickly. He pointed toward the bedchamber door that was ajar, where a shadow was moving in the candlelight.

It appeared to Kit that the shadow was in a hurry. They were moving something around the king's bedchamber, shifting things back and forth, even tying more ropes. Kit shuddered and reached for Iomhar's arm, making him lean down toward her as she whispered.

"We are beneath the queen's chambers." She did not need to say any more. If all this gunpowder went off, then the queen's rooms would be burnt to a cinder within seconds.

As one, they stepped forward, inching closer to the chamber door until the view beyond came into focus.

The bed was still made, as if the king would return. Around the bed, the curtains were tucked away within embroidered strips of linen. In front of the bed was an old coffer, this one truly ancient, for it bore the same layers of dust and webs as the other ageing furniture. Then something was kicked into view. Falling in front of the coffer was a small box, this one not so old.

A figure moved in front of the box, their back turned to the door so they were not aware of Kit's and Iomhar's presence. With their hair tucked under a yeoman guard's hat, it was impossible to discern the colour of it. The clothes did just as good a job of hiding the figure's identity as they delved a hand into the box, pulling something out from its depths. As they stood straight and walked across the chamber, Kit caught sight of more ropes hanging from their fingers. They were setting up more gunpowder.

Kit pulled on Iomhar's arm, urging him to wait. She pointed to the ropes suspended in the withdrawing chamber where they stood and began to untie them, one at a time. With quick fingers she tugged them free, so the gunpowder became disconnected, breaking the trap. Once the rope was removed completely, she tucked it away in her weapons belt, not wanting to give the culprit a chance to prime the powder again.

Iomhar clearly had no intention of waiting much longer. He walked toward the door, moving quickly and quietly, leaving Kit to hasten to his side. Stepping into the bedchamber, she almost turned dizzy at the sight.

More items of furniture had clearly been brought into this room — coffers, bible boxes, and another settle bench. There was so much that it was clear the culprit could not have acted alone. They must have had help carrying such things into the chamber.

The person in question had their back to them as they pushed another slip of rope into the bible box, so focused on the task that they didn't notice Kit and Iomhar's arrival, not until the crossbow clicked in Iomhar's hands. The figure's head jerked up, their fingers going limp around the rope.

"Turn around," Iomhar instructed, his voice so deep it echoed across the chamber.

The figure stood taller, lifting their head to reveal the full extent of the yeoman's uniform they were using as a disguise, before they turned and finally showed their face.

Kit felt her stomach knot, though she was not surprised. The pale cheeks were there, along with the blue eyes, fair hair and crooked nose. Lord Ruskin was staring at the two of them, his eyes flitting between their faces.

"Do not move, Iomhar," he said, his voice light as he gestured to the candle beside him.

Kit turned her eyes toward it, realising how Lord Ruskin had intended to set his trap and get away. A tallow candle had been lit and was burning down fast atop a candelabra. At the bottom of the wax, strands of rope were attached, so that when the wick and wax were spent, the rope would be set alight and would travel to each of the boxes. The entire chamber was tethered, ready for the impending explosion.

# CHAPTER 26

"I can always hurry the moment along," Lord Ruskin said, raising a finger and tapping the candle. The flame wobbled, threatening to topple completely.

"Then you could not escape," Kit warned.

Lord Ruskin's eyes flicked to her with pure hatred. "Would ye like to test my resolve, Miss Scarlett?" he asked, with a kind of devilish pleasure as he lifted his finger another time, threatening to push the candle over.

"Enough games," Iomhar muttered, then the crossbow clicked.

Kit was barely prepared for the whistle of the bolt through the air, before it landed in Lord Ruskin's shoulder, pushing him far away from the candle. He fell into the settle bench that was set up with rope and sprawled across the seat. His hand lifted to his right shoulder in which the bolt was embedded. He cried out like a wounded sow.

"You may have killed him," Kit said in amazement as Iomhar marched forward.

"He will live, though I hardly care if he does die after what he was trying to do. He would have contentedly watched us all burn." Iomhar attached the crossbow to his belt once more and reached toward Lord Ruskin.

Kit got to work on the room. She hurried to the tallow candle with the ropes fastened tightly around the wrought-iron holder and began to untie them. Her fingers were sweaty, making it difficult to get purchase.

"Ye bastard," Lord Ruskin cursed. "Ye could have at least made the death quick."

"Quick, eh? What good would come from that?" Iomhar grabbed hold of Lord Ruskin's injured shoulder, using it to pull him off the bench and force him to his knees on the floorboards. The man cried out in agony, with one hand pressed to the wound, trying to tear the bolt out. "Ye want to die? Pulling it free could certainly do that. It is stopping ye bleeding out."

Lord Ruskin didn't appear to believe him. He tussled beneath Iomhar, trying to break out of his hold.

"The ropes, Kit?" Iomhar called to her.

"Not safe yet." She abandoned trying to untie the knots. Her fingers were too damp with sweat. She reached for one of the daggers in her belt, lifting it free and preparing to cut the ropes.

"Tell me what I want to know." Iomhar turned back to Lord Ruskin.

"Aye, your father, again. Always about your father." Lord Ruskin's agonised words made Kit pause with the dagger. The blade was pressed to the rope when she flicked her eyes back to Iomhar and Lord Ruskin.

Iomhar was turning increasingly red in his determination to keep Lord Ruskin on his knees whilst Ruskin was becoming white, as pale as the cobwebs around them.

"Then answer me quickly," Iomhar ordered. "Ye have escaped the question long enough. Ye were there the day he died. Ye were supposed to be fighting with him, soldiers together escorting the imprisoned Mary Stuart —"

"Ye say her name?" Lord Ruskin was suddenly alert, trying even harder to wrench Iomhar off him. He managed to stand, his strength almost a match for Iomhar's.

"Kit?" Iomhar called for her help.

Kit tore the dagger through the ropes. The moment they were cut loose, she tossed the ends to the ground and kicked them away, so even if the candle fell it would not roll near enough to the ropes to set them alight. Then she moved forward to help. Grabbing Lord Ruskin's shoulders from behind, she forced him to his knees again.

"She is your queen, ye traitor," Lord Ruskin snapped, trying his best to peel Kit off his shoulders. When he reached for his weapons belt, Kit bent down and unlatched it. With a knee to his back, she made him fall forward onto his face, flat to the floorboards as she snatched the belt away. Iomhar stood back, loading the crossbow with another bolt.

When Lord Ruskin moved to his knees, the crossbow was lifted to his face and he froze, not moving an inch.

"Ye want your truth. That is why ye will not fire, Blackwood," Ruskin muttered, his voice quiet and seething.

"Then tell me quickly," Iomhar said, pushing the crossbow forward. "Or shall I shoot the other shoulder?"

Lord Ruskin flinched. "It was war. A soldier killed a soldier. That is what I told ye before, and I will tell ye again."

Kit stepped away and looked around the room, feeling sickened to the core. She rather suspected that this was how Lord Ruskin saw every day of his life, as a war, a constant battle to achieve one aim. He had planted an obscene amount of gunpowder, designed to not only kill one woman whilst she slept, but also her friends, her staff, and her council. It was brutal and malicious.

"This is murder," she said aloud. "This is not war." She gestured to the room, watching as Lord Ruskin lifted his eyes to her. He placed a hand over his injured shoulder, holding onto the bolt. "Is that what you saw today as? Another death in a war?"

"We soldiers are the bringers of death, Miss Scarlett." He tipped his chin high, seeming proud. "Something this traitor should have known, as his father before him should have done."

Iomhar lifted the crossbow, but Kit stepped forward and stopped him from firing. Iomhar raised his green gaze to her, wide with alarm.

"Kit, this has to be done. He knows what happened that day."

"Then find another way to ask him," she replied, remembering their conversation in Northumberland. "Like Luca, he is not a man who will answer your question because of pain. Torture does no good."

Iomhar's grasp on the crossbow loosened as he recognised the truth. Kit stepped back, allowing him to finish. Within minutes they would need to arrest Lord Ruskin, and Iomhar had been waiting years to ask these questions.

"I wouldn't have thought it would come to this anyway," he said with a scoff, gesturing to the bolt in Lord Ruskin's shoulder. "Ye have always spoken of a soldier's duty to fight, to cause death. Are ye not proud of what happened the day my father was killed?"

Kit hid her smile as she turned away, for Iomhar was appealing to Lord Ruskin's vanity. He clearly wanted to talk of the great things he had done in the name of his queen. His spine straightened as he sat there on his knees.

"Aye, I am proud."

"Then tell me why ye are proud," Iomhar ordered, stepping toward him again. "My father was trying to escort Mary Stuart from one house arrest to the next."

"The Queen of Scots!"

"Mary Stuart," Iomhar retorted, refusing to address her as a queen at all. "Ye stopped her movement. Ye were there with your soldiers; ye saw my father and his battalion attacked. Who killed my father?"

"It was an order!" Lord Ruskin barked as he took hold of the bolt again.

Kit noted the way he gritted his teeth as he tried to pull the bolt free, practically drawing blood from his gums. Iomhar inched forward, his body buckling with the strain of his own wound as he placed a hand to his side.

"What did ye say?" Iomhar demanded. "Someone ordered his death? Who? Who ordered his death? Was it ye?"

"I am a soldier. I am not the commander!"

Kit stepped back, knowing who in that castle was considered a commander. The woman that Lord Ruskin and his men would have obeyed more than any other.

"Iomhar," she said softly, reaching for his arm.

"Not now, Kit. I want to hear it." He bent down to Lord Ruskin. As Ruskin took hold of the bolt, trying to tear it free, Iomhar stopped him, holding on to the other end and making the man cry out. "Ye want it free? Then tell me. Who ordered my father's death?"

"Who do ye think?" Lord Ruskin snapped wildly, lifting his chin so high that it nearly met Iomhar's. "Who did not want him watching over her anymore? Who knew that as long as he was there, the soldiers would listen to him and not her? The Earl of Ross always had loyalty, didn't he? Even when that loyalty should have been to the queen herself!"

Kit lifted a hand and covered her mouth, stunned at the revelation. Iomhar appeared to receive the news with equal incredulity. He shook his head a little.

"Nay, that cannot be. Ye are telling me that she…"

"Aye, our queen ordered your father's death. Repayment for him being a traitor, being one of the men who put her son on the throne instead of her." Lord Ruskin held his gaze as he spoke.

Iomhar released the bolt and stood, turning away. When Kit reached out to him, he stumbled away from her, leaning on the nearest wall, as if he had been struck in the gut and winded by the news.

Kit took out the ropes from her weapons belt, shifting them toward Lord Ruskin.

"Don't tie me up like an animal."

"You do not get to make that choice." She walked around him and moved his hands behind his back, having to wrench one of them free of the bolt. He cried out as she forced his hands further up his back and looped the rope around his wrists.

"Who followed the order?" Iomhar asked, jerking out of his daze.

"Iomhar..." Kit began slowly.

"I have to know." He turned to face Ruskin. "Who followed the order?" His voice was louder this time.

Kit hadn't expected Ruskin to lift his chin higher. The sudden movement tore his wrists from her grasp before she could fasten his hands tightly together. He reached behind, grabbing her and forcing her to the ground.

"Kit!" Iomhar called as she felt a blade pushed to her back. It only took a second for Kit to realise that Ruskin had snatched the dagger from her belt.

"Nay further," Lord Ruskin warned. Kit could see Iomhar's boots as they were forced to retreat across the room. When she felt the dagger pierce the thick material of her doublet, she held her breath. "I always follow my queen's orders, Iomhar. Something ye and your father should have done."

Kit closed her eyes, despairing as she realised the horrid truth. The man whom Iomhar had been hunting — the man he believed knew the secret of his father's death — was the very man who had committed the murder.

"Ye bastard," Iomhar muttered.

"Your father said that."

The conversation was too distracting for Lord Ruskin to be focused on what he was doing. Kit took the opportunity. She rolled her body to the side with sudden speed, taking the dagger in her doublet with her. It scraped along the floorboards but could not pierce her. Lord Ruskin fell over her in the sudden scuffle, allowing her to thrust up with her knee, striking him in the gut and forcing him away from her.

Kit moved to her feet as Iomhar leapt forward, his crossbow raised in Lord Ruskin's direction. Ruskin lashed out, kicking Kit in the chest and forcing her backwards. Iomhar dropped the crossbow and hurried to catch her instead.

The two of them ended up on the floor with his arms under her. His cry showed how much pain it had caused him to fall in this way with his wound still so recent. Kit rolled off him as her eyes shot to Lord Ruskin. He picked up the tallow candle, rushing toward the door before dropping the flame to the floor.

"Goodbye, Blackwood, Miss Scarlett."

As the flame fell toward the bundle of ropes Kit had pushed to the side earlier, Ruskin escaped, darting out of the room.

"Kit, the ropes!" Iomhar shouted.

"I see them!" she cried back, scrambling on her hands and knees. She pulled them out of the boxes as quickly as possible. The settle bench was first, then a coffer and a bible box, making each one safe, but the flames were getting away from her.

She was no longer chasing just one flame, for the rope had split into a myriad of threads across the room, each one ending up in a different vessel of gunpowder.

"Kit!" Iomhar called. She turned, seeing him holding her dagger that he had found on the floor. He slid it across the floorboards, struggling to get to his feet with the pain in his side.

Kit snatched it up and cut the ropes, a few at a time until they were nearly all done.

"Ye missed one!" Iomhar snapped, thrusting a finger across the room.

On her feet, Kit fell, slipping over some of the ropes in her effort to reach the final one. She barely managed to pull the rope out of the coffer in time, tugging the thread down so that it fell on her doublet and lit the material there. She clapped her palm to her chest repeatedly, snuffing out the flame before the material could take light. Then, the only sounds in the room were their heavy breaths as they gazed around.

"That was…"

"Aye, it was," Iomhar agreed as he struggled to his feet, wincing. "Ruskin…" He tried to stagger to the door.

"Iomhar?" Kit called after him. She bundled the last of the ropes together, tearing them free so that no one could return to light them. She then ran from the room, hurrying after Iomhar. She found him in the privy chamber, half collapsed against the table. "You are in no fit state to go after him."

"Then ye go after him!" He motioned madly toward the door, but they both froze as they heard glass shattering nearby.

Kit moved to the one window in the room and peered beyond. She could just about see someone who had broken a window and was climbing down a wall, with a rope tethering him to the top. When he reached the outer wall of the palace, he walked along it before leaping down the other side, disappearing from view.

"Iomhar, he's…"

"I know." Iomhar's voice was close by. Kit turned to see him standing beside her, reaching out a hand to lean on the windowsill. "He has gone. He will have a horse, a cart, even a boat or something waiting for him. There is nay chance to catch him now."

Kit had no words as Iomhar leaned against the wall. She had never had family, so she could not imagine what Iomhar was going through having learned that Lord Ruskin was his father's killer.

She did the only thing she could do and placed her hand over his arm. He held onto it as if it was the last thing keeping him standing.

# CHAPTER 27

"It is safe, Your Majesty." Kit let the words settle in the room. The queen moved toward the edge of the chair where she was resting, with Lady Hunsdon on one side of her and Lady Stafford on the other, clutching her hand. In the doorway beside Kit was Iomhar, leaning on the doorframe with a hand to his side. Walsingham was standing apart from the queen and listening to Kit with equally rapt attention.

"What has happened?" the queen asked quietly.

"Lord Ruskin filled the king's chambers with gunpowder," Kit said. "It seems he wished to drive you back to your chamber tonight, Your Majesty. He did not just want you to die, but your friends too, in the hope that it would destroy this monarchy."

Walsingham rubbed a hand against the bridge of his nose as the queen sat back, her body slumped.

"What of Lord Ruskin?" At her question, Kit and Iomhar exchanged a look, their silence the only answer she needed. "I see. He has escaped. Have the yeomen not caught him? What of the gentlemen-at-arms?"

"They didn't think to stop one dressed as their own," Iomhar explained slowly, prompting the queen to scoff and hold her friend's hand more tightly.

"He must be found." The queen's voice shook as she turned her gaze on Kit. "Miss Scarlett, there must be something…?"

"We have sent people to look for him, but I fear Lord Ruskin has friends." Kit's mind turned back to the furniture. If Lord Ruskin had enough associates in London, then they could have all crept into the palace dressed as yeomen to help move the supposed gifts to the queen. "With his plan thwarted, I think he will have retreated from London before sunrise with their help."

The queen nodded, trying to look composed, but her hands gave her away. One of them was gripping the maid's skirt she still wore, as Miss Parry laid a fine shawl around her shoulders.

"That is all we can do for now, it seems." The queen's gaze darted to Walsingham, silently communicating that their conversation was not over. She then addressed Kit and Iomhar once more. "The gunpowder? It is safe?"

"Yes, Your Majesty," Iomhar answered. "It is being taken from the room now by the intelligencers. Your chamber will be safe to return to soon."

"You think I wish to return?" The queen shook her head. "I have no wish for the memory of these last few weeks to revisit me. Walsingham, prepare our departure for Richmond, if you will."

"Yes, of course." Walsingham bowed and turned to walk past Kit and Iomhar, stopping between them momentarily. "Come to me tomorrow morning at Seething Lane. There is much we need to discuss." With one final nod at Kit, he was gone. It was a brief mark of respect, the only acknowledgement she would get that she had accomplished their task that night.

As Walsingham disappeared down the corridor, Kit turned back to the queen, seeing that she was shakily standing. Lady Hunsdon and Lady Stafford went with her, each holding her up as she advanced toward Kit. As the queen stopped in front of her, Kit curtsied, breaking the eye contact.

"Is this a victory, I wonder?" the queen murmured.

"You are alive, Your Majesty. That is most certainly a victory," said Kit.

"For today. We shall have to see about tomorrow." The queen gave her first smile of the evening. "Thank you, Miss Scarlett. Thanks to you, I have defied death again." She flicked her eyes around the room with apparent distaste. "I have never liked it here, and now I have cause to like it even less. Anne, let us prepare to part." Once more her voice was formidable and strong, though her body still needed assistance to move.

Kit and Iomhar stepped to the side and let the queen depart, followed by all the ladies. Once the last one had gone, they stood opposite each other, either side of the doorframe. Kit could not decipher Iomhar's expression. It was dark, but there seemed to be relief there too.

"Iomhar?" she said quietly, capturing his attention. "Are you well?" She gestured to his side.

"The wound is fine. Aye, I am well." He sighed and leaned against the doorframe. "We came close tonight, Kit. A wee bit too close. A minute longer and we would not be standing here to talk of it."

She chewed her lip, knowing he was right. Lord Ruskin was not going to be cowed.

Kit stepped away from the doorframe, ready to leave, but she noticed Iomhar didn't follow her. He stayed in position for a minute, until Kit stepped back toward him and offered her hand. He took it silently as they walked slowly down the corridor.

"Kitty, you will have to wait to see Walsingham." Doris beckoned Kit in through the door, closing it hurriedly behind her and sliding the numerous locks. "He has someone with him right now."

"I can wait," Kit murmured, glancing ahead to the empty corridor and the staircase that led to Walsingham's room. If

Walsingham was busy, then it gave her the chance to act on an idea she'd had. Somewhere in Seething Lane, there had to be some proof of who she'd once been.

As Doris finished securing all the locks, a loud clatter ricocheted through the house. Kit reached for her belt, placing a hand on the hilt of her dagger as Doris reached for her and laughed.

"Oh, do not worry yourself, Kitty. No great mystery about what that sound is." Doris beckoned Kit to follow her, pointing into the kitchen nearby. A young girl held a copper pot in one hand, and the handle in the other. "My new kitchen maid. My bones have grown weary these days, and the master agreed to pay for a helping hand, though how much help she is proving to be…"

"I am sorry, miss," the young girl said hurriedly, chewing her lip as she looked down at the two pieces of the copper pot.

"That will not do for a cooking pot now, will it?" Doris said impatiently. "Come, I'll show you where we keep the spares." As Doris waved the maid out through the other kitchen door, opposite to where Kit stood, she glanced back and tutted, earning a soft laugh.

Kit watched them go, waiting until all she could hear were their murmurs in the distance. Once she was far enough away to be certain she could sneak through the house unnoticed, she dropped a bag from her shoulder and pushed it into the corner of the house, beside the front door, half hidden by the shadows and cloths that hung down off the kitchen door.

Glancing back to ensure that whoever was with Walsingham had not yet left, Kit took off through the kitchen, following the path Doris had taken into the furthest regions of the house. On the other side, Kit reached a small spiral staircase, closed off from the corridor by a narrow door. Lifting the black iron latch, she hid herself inside, having to squeeze into the space.

When she'd been a child, Walsingham had jested that it was her own personal staircase, for only those as small as her could easily use it to reach the lofts of the house. These days, Kit was too tall, having to bend down to stop herself from hitting her head on the stonework. Passing windows so small that they were barely wider than the span of her hand, she hurried to the top of the house, walking on the balls of her feet.

She passed by three doors in the staircase before she found the one that she was looking for, pulling the door to the loft open. It swung with a creak before Kit stepped inside and closed it tightly behind her.

The room was not as she remembered it. Before she had taken her own lodgings in town, this space had been her home. Now, the bed had been replaced with a desk that no one seemed to use. The coffer was still there, but when she lifted the lid Kit found none of her clothes inside it. It was a storage space for tallow candles and bedsheets. Closing the coffer once more, Kit looked around the room, trying to think of any moment in her childhood that had involved some sort of secret place.

She could easily recall the way Walsingham had stridden across the room when she had sat in the middle of the floor. It had been one of the first days she had worn a hose and doublet, and she'd been trying to decode a slip of parchment in her lap, with her tongue between her teeth. "This room is yours, Kit," he'd said. "I want you to treat it as such."

The memory of the words made Kit hurry back to the door, thinking herself a fool. If Walsingham was indeed trying to hide something from her, then he was hardly going to keep it in the very room he had given to her.

She crept back down the narrow staircase, listening carefully at the doors on each level to ensure Doris and the kitchen maid were elsewhere in the house. When their voices passed close by the door that led to the main landing, Kit stayed still. The voices soon moved on, disappearing into other rooms, giving Kit the opportunity that she needed.

Peeling the door open a crack, she poked her head through the gap to check the landing. There was no Doris, no maid, no Walsingham and none of his secretaries. Far ahead at the distant end of the corridor was the firmly closed door of Walsingham's chamber. Kit could remember reaching up to the doorhandle on her tiptoes when she'd been very little, trying to get inside. Walsingham had stopped her, firmly telling her that the room was out of bounds.

"If he is hiding something, it will be in here," she whispered to herself. Glancing once more up and down the corridor, she hastened toward the door and unlatched the handle easily, slipping inside as quickly as she could.

Scents struck her as she closed the door, forcing Kit to squint and clutch her nose, peering up at the ceiling. She was reminded of the queen's chamber and the way the apothecary had draped herbs around the place, trying to ward off evils and infections. Over the bed and across the window there were multiple bundles of green leaves gathered, and there was a large posy standing on a table with a washbasin next to it. The watery scent of borage hung in the air, along with the sweet smell of cleavers.

Kit shivered, realising the true state of Walsingham's health. He had claimed repeatedly to her that the fire in Seething Lane had caused him no lasting damage, but he had been ill before that, and what exactly the cause was, he would never tell her.

But she knew about the back pains, the tiredness, and the way he clung to his mercury pills, as if they were the giver of life.

Stumbling forward, she covered her nose completely, trying to block out the scent. Reaching toward the far side of the room, she acted quickly, pulling open two coffers and searching the depths. She pushed past cloaks and jerkins, all either black or of equally dark hues. Recognising nothing from her dream, she closed the coffers quickly and turned to a vast wardrobe, dark oak with arches carved into the wood and small curving blossoms that formed the wrought-iron handles.

At first, she could see nothing inside but more black garments. She pushed them to the side impatiently, turning her gaze downward. Pressed into the far corner, behind rows of shoes that had all been lined up obsessively neatly, there was a small carved box. Made of the same dark oak as the wardrobe, it almost disappeared into the shadows and Kit would have missed it had she not brushed her knuckles against it.

Glancing toward the chamber door to check no one was nearby, she lifted the box out of the wardrobe and laid it on the floorboards. She was ready to prise the lid open when she found a tiny metal lock pushed through a clasp at the front.

"So secretive, Walsingham. I should have known," she whispered to herself, reaching for her belt. She didn't have time to search for a key, and she knew Walsingham would have made it very difficult to find. Pulling one of the daggers out of her belt, she slipped the thin blade through the hoop of the padlock and levered it open. It only took two attempts; the lock was so small and fiddly that it broke into two shards. Stuffing the dagger into her belt, she lifted the lid, pausing when the dim light from the windows fell on the contents of the box.

Silk stared up at her, pale pink and damaged in sections. Kit lifted it up by the shoulders, revealing a small gown made for a child. She blinked, not wanting to believe she had seen it before, but she had.

In that dream where she was in the water, so small that her pudgy hands could not reach the surface, she could remember looking down at her feet to where stockings were slipping off her toes. The pink gown was also memorable, with the pearl beads that sat around the neckline. Kit ran a finger along the pearls, remembering seeing them just beneath her chin.

Nausea washed over her. Kit dropped the gown into the box and scrambled backward.

"It is true," Kit murmured. "So God mend me." She lowered her forehead to the floorboards as if in prayer, though she could not pray. She could only grit her teeth together in anger.

The dream was no dream, just as she had suspected. It was a memory, and not only had Walsingham lied about it for years on end, but he had also kept the gown that she had been wearing.

Sickened, she sat up and snatched the gown. For some reason, she couldn't leave it here. She was going to challenge Walsingham; she needed to know why she had been wearing such a dress and why she'd been drowning.

Moving to her knees, Kit tucked the gown under her arm and stuffed the broken padlock into the box, then returned it to the corner of the wardrobe.

# CHAPTER 28

Doris was off somewhere in the belly of the house, her voice reaching Kit's ears every now and then, but there was no one else nearby. At least, there wasn't for a while. The dress was still hanging half in and out of Kit's bag when the door to Walsingham's room on the upper floor opened and closed, followed by fast footsteps on the staircase, leading down to the corridor where Kit stood.

As soon as the last folds of the silk dress had been pushed deep into the bag, she closed the leather flap and kicked it toward the door. She then spun round and walked down the corridor.

Iomhar stepped off the staircase, appearing in front of her. For a minute he stared at the floorboards, his face wan and his eyes wide.

"You met a ghost?" Kit asked, approaching him.

He snapped his gaze up to meet hers, clearly surprised to find her there. "Nay, nothing like that." He shook his head.

"I did not know you were already here. I am guessing you have seen Walsingham. Do we have a new commission?" she asked, aware that Iomhar didn't seem to be his usual self. "Iomhar? Is something wrong?"

"It is hard to put into words."

"If it is Lord Ruskin —"

"It's not him." Iomhar spoke quickly, cutting her off.

"It is not?" Kit asked, closing the distance between them. "Because we will find him."

"Will we?" Iomhar asked, his expression dubious.

"We will keep looking. He seems to have a habit of making himself known, too. I wouldn't wonder if he turned up in London once more, sooner than you think." Kit found his silence unsettling, so she just kept speaking. "How is the wound?" she asked. "Have you recovered a little more? You are standing straight now, which is more than you were doing before. You looked rather like you had a hunchback, unable to stand tall at all —"

"Kit?"

"Yes?" she said, looking up as Iomhar interrupted her.

"Ye are prattling." He spoke softly with a small smile, seeming thoroughly amused by the idea.

"Can you blame me?" she asked with a shrug. "You are not saying anything much at all."

"Nay, I am stuck with my thoughts." His face contorted, as if he was in pain. "Do me a favour and be quiet for one moment."

"As you wish." She nodded and went to place her hands on her hips, but Iomhar caught her right hand in his and brought it swiftly upwards, pressing his lips to the back. Kit was unprepared for it, and her jaw fell open. She stared at him, aware that his green eyes never left her as he held that kiss. "You and I do not normally do this," she whispered.

"Plenty do," he murmured, lifting his lips, though he didn't quite lower her hand. "It is the formal thing, is it not? For men and women to greet each other and part in this way."

"Formal?" She nearly spluttered in surprise. "You did not do that so formally."

"Perhaps not." He lifted her hand and kissed it again. This time, Kit clamped her lips shut, attempting to control the thudding in her chest. When he stopped that kiss, he lowered her hand between the two of them, not releasing it.

"What was that for?" Kit whispered.

"I am not certain how else to say this." Iomhar sighed and looked down at their connected hands.

Kit held her breath, thinking of all the implications that Walsingham had made, and the friction that had been between her and Iomhar lately. The comments he had made about her shrinking from his touch had lingered too. She waited for him to make some sort of confession, anything to reveal what he truly thought of her, even though he couldn't look at her.

"It is time to say goodbye, Kit."

She blinked, dumbstruck. When Iomhar said nothing more and only continued to stare at her hand, Kit pulled on his fingers, needing him to look her in the eye. "What did you say?" she asked quietly. "Did you say goodbye?"

"Aye, Kit. Goodbye." His voice was barely above a whisper.

"What? No." She shook her head, too confused to be able to form a coherent sentence. "What do you mean, goodbye? You mean goodbye as in, I will see you tomorrow, or…"

"I mean I do not know when I will see ye next." He spoke firmly, never blinking, leaving her standing perfectly still with an increasingly dry mouth. She swallowed before she attempted to speak.

"What has happened?" Kit flicked her gaze toward the staircase that led to Walsingham's room. "Has Walsingham done this? Is he sending you away?"

"There is a commission that must be done," Iomhar said calmly, still holding onto her hand. "Walsingham has insisted that I am the man to do it."

"You mean he has ordered you to go? To leave London?" Kit could feel the certainty of it, without Iomhar having to tell her as much. The warning Walsingham had uttered when

Iomhar had been unconscious was fresh in her mind. "If you have a commission, then I should come with you."

"Nay," Iomhar said so quickly that she flinched.

"What do you mean 'nay'?" she mimicked, pulling a momentary smile to his lips.

"Nay, Kit. Walsingham has told me I must go alone. Ye are needed here."

"Here? Why?"

"By the sounds of things, our queen has taken a liking to the spy that dresses as a man. She thinks ye keep her safe." Iomhar shrugged, his tone light for a few seconds. "Aye, she is a good judge of character after all."

"Where are you going?"

"I cannot tell ye."

"What do you mean by that?" Kit asked impatiently, her hand closing tighter around his.

"As pleased as I am to see ye nay longer hide from my touch, ye do not need to bruise me," he muttered playfully.

"Iomhar."

"I know," he whispered. "I cannot tell ye where I am going as he has ordered me not to."

"That is absurd. Since when do you obey his orders to the letter?" Kit asked, glancing toward the staircase again.

"On this occasion, I'll follow them. I think it wise ye do not know."

The words made her look back at him sharply. "When do you leave?" she asked softly.

"Today, almost this moment."

"No." Kit found the word falling from her lips as she shook her head and looked down at their hands. He seemed to be equally reluctant to let go.

"Aye, Kit. I have to."

Silence fell between them. Kit couldn't look up into his face, half scared of the expression she would find there. She chewed her lip instead, staring down at his hand on hers. Iomhar shifted, entwining their fingers together.

"There, nay longer running from me," he whispered.

"You are the one running now," Kit replied quietly. When she at last looked up at him, she noted his pained expression as he lifted his free hand to his jaw, scratching his cropped beard. "When will you come back?" The silence stretched out, making Kit panic. "Iomhar, tell me you are coming back."

"We will see."

"Are you intending to be cryptic?"

"I must be, Kit. It is necessary." His tone was as firm as her own, not faltering for a second.

She parted her lips to argue with him some more, but he simply raised his eyebrows. "You will not tell me what is going on, will you? No matter what I ask you."

"See? Ye know me well after all."

In the distance, a door opened and closed.

"Someone is coming," Kit whispered. She went to remove her hand from Iomhar's, but he didn't let it go. "Tell me something of where you are going, anything at all," she begged, glancing over her shoulder. It sounded like Doris in the distance, perhaps murmuring with the new kitchen maid.

"As ye wish," Iomhar said, speaking quickly. "Before I follow Walsingham's orders, my family needs to hear of what happened with Lord Ruskin. I'll go to them first in the Highlands. Then I will do as Walsingham asks of me."

"Then I could —"

"Nay."

"You do not even know what I was about to say," Kit said, glancing behind her once more.

"Ye were going to offer to come with me. Ye are needed here, Kit. The queen has asked for it."

"Doris is coming," Kit murmured.

"Then this is goodbye," Iomhar whispered. He lifted her hand to his lips and kissed it again. He held that kiss for a beat longer and then lowered her hand, just as Doris appeared at the end of the corridor. Iomhar stood back and smiled at Kit without vigour or enthusiasm, then he left, walking by her in such a way that his arm brushed hers, making her shiver.

Kit turned, ready to follow him when she saw Doris and the kitchen maid walking her way.

"All well, Kitty?" Doris asked jovially.

"Y-yes, thank you," Kit stammered, watching as Iomhar hesitated in the doorway. He glanced back at her once, winked, and then he was gone, with the door closing behind him.

"Are you certain, Kitty?" Doris asked, touching Kit's shoulder.

Kit couldn't answer this time. She looked away from Doris, the kitchen maid, and the closed door, before hurrying off toward the staircase. She took the steps two at a time in her eagerness to reach the very top, before knocking impatiently on the door.

"God's blood, what are you doing and who are you?" Walsingham cried out.

Kit pushed open the door, striding in with such vigour that she rather expected to punch holes through the floorboards with the heels of her boots.

"Kit? That sounded more like a musket going off than a knock. What is wrong with —"

"Where have you sent Iomhar?" Kit asked, cutting Walsingham off.

He was standing in the middle of his room, with some papers in his hands. Her question silenced him, and his lips pressed together in a firm line.

"Walsingham?" She urged him, speaking louder this time, "Where have you sent him?"

"Well, I'm pleased to see the man keeps to his vows. I made him promise not to tell you where he was going. I must admit, I was not confident he would keep the secret." He turned to the fireplace and dropped a slip of parchment on the fire. Kit's eyes darted toward it, recognising the mark of a unicorn in the corner, along with some scrawled lettering. Any chance she had of reading more vanished as the parchment was set alight. The pale paper curled into a bright yellow and orange flame, dancing back and forth like a jester at court.

"Why would you do that?" Kit asked, following Walsingham toward the fireplace.

"Kit, may I remind you that you both work for me. You are both my intelligencers, and where I send one, I do not have to tell the other."

"You are the one who made us work together. Since that day, we have not worked apart."

"That was my own mistake."

"What mistake?"

"Kit, that is enough." Walsingham held up a hand. "He is gone. Let that be the end of the matter."

"The end of what, precisely? When is he coming back?" Kit asked. Her words seemed to anger Walsingham so much that his eyes bulged.

"Why do you care so much, Kit?"

"He is my friend."

Walsingham shook his head. "He is more than that to you, and we both know it."

"We rely on each other. That is what happens when you work together in this way."

"To the point that I saw you in tears when you thought his life was in danger?"

"I would call that a human response," Kit spat in her fury. She turned away from Walsingham, realising she was getting nowhere, and ran her hands through her hair.

"Yes, perfectly human, especially for someone who is so attached to another!" He was shouting at her as if she were a child again, running and skulking in the attics of Seething Lane.

"What is so wrong with being attached to him?" Kit asked, spinning on the heel of her boot to face him.

"It makes for a poor intelligencer, Kit." Walsingham marched toward her, barking the words and waving the papers he was clutching toward her chest. "You need to have no attachments, no loyalty to anyone but the queen and I. You need to be able to go anywhere and turn away from anyone when asked."

Kit shook her head, struggling for words as her body thrummed with anger, her heart racing. "You have sent him away because you did not like the fact that I was attached to Iomhar? Is that all it was?"

"No." Walsingham turned, pushing another of the papers into the fire. "A commission arose. Iomhar is the best one to take it, of that I give you my word, Kit."

"Then what is the point of this conversation? All this talk of attachments?" Kit scoffed.

"The commission has two merits. Iomhar takes the commission, and the two of you are parted," Walsingham said decisively, leaning on the mantelpiece over the fire as he dropped the last of the paperwork into the grate. "You and

Iomhar need some time apart. It is good for both of you. To break this ... bond."

Kit breathed deeply and sharply, trying to calm herself. "When will he come back?" she whispered after a minute of silence.

"I do not know." Walsingham's voice was so dark that she snapped her gaze toward him.

"Does that mean he is not coming back at all?"

Walsingham didn't answer her. He leaned across the mantelpiece and picked up a sheet of folded parchment that he had placed behind an iron paperweight.

"You have your orders," he said, walking toward her with the letter in his grasp. "The queen has sent a message for you."

"For me?" Kit asked, standing taller.

"She wants you to go to her. Now." Walsingham pushed the letter toward her. "Do yourself a kindness, Kit. Take this letter, go to see your queen and forget about Iomhar Blackwood. Will you do that?"

Kit stood motionless for a minute, until she saw Walsingham tilt his head, watching her as a red kite watched its prey.

She took the letter from him and turned to the door.

# A NOTE TO THE READER

Dear Reader,

Thank you for taking the time to read the third in the series of Kit Scarlett's adventures.

The inspiration for Kit's tale comes from a longing to see more stories where women are at the centre of a tale that is truly adventurous. We know from hints of this time period that there was the occasional woman doing espionage, but with Kit, I've taken that idea and thrown her completely into this world. Not only is she a spy, fighting to defend her queen in one of the most turbulent times of history, when there were often attempts on the queen's life, but Kit is in the deep end. It is her responsibility to see that the queen stays safe.

Naturally, at times, fact is played with a little and people are invented. The purpose of this book is to entertain, after all, so I hope I have indeed done that, and you have enjoyed this story as much as I enjoyed writing it. This is a created world, where a woman walks freely dressed as a man, saving lives and even the country, but who knows? This is a world of shadows, where intelligencers operated in the dark and, for all we know, a woman like Kit may have truly existed.

Reviews by readers these days are integral to a book's success, so if you enjoyed Kit's tale I would be very grateful if you could spare a minute to post a review on **Amazon** and **Goodreads**. I love hearing from readers, and you can talk with me through **my website** or **on Twitter** and follow my author page **on Facebook**.

I hope we'll meet again on Kit's next adventure.

Adele Jordan

**Sapere Books** is an exciting new publisher of brilliant fiction and popular history.

To find out more about our latest releases and our monthly bargain books visit our website: **saperebooks.com**

www.ingramcontent.com/pod-product-compliance
Lightning Source LLC
LaVergne TN
LVHW051516070426
835507LV00023B/3136